WILEY ONLINE TRADING FOR A LIVING

Electronic Day Trading to Win / Bob Baird and Craig McBurney

The Strategic Electronic Day Trader / Robert Deel

Day Trade Online / Christopher A. Farrell

Trade Options Online / George A. Fontanills

Electronic Day Trading 101 / Sunny J. Harris

How I Trade for a Living / Gary Smith

the
strategic
electronic
day
trader

the strategic electronic day trader

ROBERT DEEL

John Wiley & Sons, Inc.

New York • Chichester • Weinheim • Brisbane • Singapore • Toronto

Published by John Wiley & Sons, Inc.
Published simultaneously in Canada.

This publication is designed to provide accurate and authoritative information in regard to the subject matter covered. It is sold with the understanding that the publisher is not engaged in rendering professional services. If professional advice or other expert assistance is required, the services of a competent professional person should be sought.

RealTick™ is a trademark of Townsend Analytics, Ltd. © 1986–1999 Townsend Analytics. Used with permission. Any unauthorized reproduction, alteration or use of RealTick™ is strictly prohibited. Authorized use of RealTick™ by John Wiley & Sons does not constitute an endorsement by Townsend Analytics of the information contained in **The Strategic Electronic Day Trader**. Townsend Analytics does not guarantee the accuracy of or warrant any representations made by **The Strategic Electronic Day Trader** of the truth or accuracy of any information written in **The Strategic Electronic Day Trader.**

Library of Congress Cataloging-in-Publication Data:
Deel, Robert.
  The strategic electronic day trader / Robert Deel.
    p.   cm.
  Includes index.
  ISBN 0-471-25488-6 (cloth : alk. paper)
    1. Day trading (Securities).   2. Electronic trading of securities.   3. Stocks—Data processing.   I. Title.

  HG4515.95.D428 2000
  332.64'0285—dc21   99-055629

Printed in the United States of America.

10 9 8 7 6 5 4 3 2 1

contents

the
strategic
electronic
day
trader

chapter 1

the dream and the reality

The Dream

Each of us has a dream. For the active student of the market there is only one: to pit his or her ability and capital against the market and earn a living from it.

For years Bill had dreamed of trading and living his dream. At age 33, he sold his printing business, making a $180,000 after-tax profit. This capital would enable him to begin living the dream, or so he thought. Four months after beginning to trade at a local electronic trading firm, Bill had lost $65,000; 63.89 percent of his trading capital had disappeared. What had taken him years to earn was gone. Bill's dream was rapidly becoming a nightmare.

The grim reality is that short-term trading—especially day trading—can be hazardous to your wealth and that 92 percent of day traders lose money in their first two years of trading. Only 8 percent are successful. Of that 8 percent, only 2 percent of the day trading *public* make money on a consistent basis. Why is it that the public gravitates toward short-term trading? There are several answers to this question. For now, let us address a more obvious question. Why do 92 percent of day traders fail, and what makes 8 percent successful? This book answers the questions and misconceptions about short-term trading. It delivers powerful trading methodology, screening procedures, tactics, and a revolutionary approach to developing emotional control and mental focus.

The Reality of the Awakening

Fortunately, Bill woke up from his nightmare and began to ask himself some profound questions. Realizing that the problem was one of his own creation, he took responsibility for his dilemma. Bill began to seek the answers he needed, which ultimately led him to tradingschool.com. After I spoke with him, it became obvious that Bill had fallen into the "traders trap." The following is the essence of our conversation, which in turn led Bill to escape from the trap he had created for himself.

We go to school, gain an education, become employed, or start our own business. We learn what we need to know to be successful, but nothing in our education or work experience provides the comprehensive knowledge or psychological control necessary for success as a trader. Bill was intelligent, he owned his own business, and he was successful. He had the money he needed to begin his dream and some experience in the stock market. Bill was the very definition of a winner, so why had he lost 63.89 percent of his capital in four months?

Unfortunately, it's human nature to assume that if we succeed in one area we will automatically succeed in another. The drive and determination that helped you succeed becomes the little voice in your head that says, "Trading and the concepts behind it seem simple enough to me. This can't be as difficult as starting and developing my own business. After that experience, I can do anything." Unfortunately, most people who enter the market with the idea of becoming traders have a feeling of invincibility, superiority, and no clue of what they are about to experience.

Bill had a college education and years of experience in the printing business before he started his own business. Even with his education and experience, Bill told me that it had been difficult, but he prevailed and became successful. With this information as background, I asked Bill a few questions. Put yourself in Bill's place and answer the following questions:

1. Would you buy a business if you had no idea what the cash flow would be?
2. Would you buy a business if you had little actual experience or training compared to your competition?
3. Would you buy a business if your competition were well capitalized and you had limited operating capital?
4. Last, but certainly not least, would you buy a business without a business plan?

If you are saying, "Not a chance," guess again. That is exactly what you are doing when you start trading for the first time. You must prepare yourself and realize that as a short-term trader you are up against the best traders in the world.

Training, experience, psychological control, and a realization that you are not invincible or smarter than the market will lead to success. Each morning before you begin to trade, say the following: "My name is (your name). I can and may lose money today, but if I trade the plan and follow the rules I will be a winner." I repeat this little saying every morning before beginning to trade. It accomplishes two things. First, it is humbling to acknowledge that the market is all powerful and can take money from you at any time. Nothing will cause you to lose money faster than a big ego or trying to exact revenge on the market. If you are trying to prove you are right all the time, you are going to lose. When you do lose, are you going to get even with the market by showing it who's boss in the next trade? Thirty minutes later you have four consecutive losses and you are still blaming the market. Another trap is trying to set a dollar amount per month or per year that you want to earn from the market. Some use a percentage—for example, they may want to earn a return of 20 percent a month. Most novice traders look at trading as an escape from a job they hate, and they know they have to make X amount of money to pay the bills. You don't need the added pressure of a monetary figure hanging over your head. This can become a psychological guillotine. If you don't meet your goal, you will push your trading beyond your skill, and the result will be a series of losses. Losing emotional control will result in large, uncontrolled losses. If you follow your trading plan, success should be the result. By focusing on your trading plan, emotion, ego, and making money are no longer an issue. If you follow your trading plan, you are a winner regardless of the monetary outcome. Knowing yourself and adopting the right mind-set, trading strategy, and methodology *before* you start trading will enable you to avoid the traders trap and begin living the dream.

Living the Dream

Dreaming the dream and living it are two different things. One is based on fantasy and the other on reality. To live the dream, you have come to the realization that short trading is like nothing you have ever experienced. The reality is that short-term trading is going to be one of the hardest things you have ever done, and without the proper training and psychological preparation, your stress level will most likely be off the scale. Mental training and conditioning will be discussed later in Chapter 7.

Living the dream successfully depends to a great extent on you—and what kind of short-term trader you are. Identifying what kind of short-term trader you are is critical to your entire trading plan. I have trained over 4,000 individual traders from all over the world. This group includes professional traders, hedge fund managers, mutual fund managers, and the general public. The first two questions I ask are as follows:

1. What kind of predator are you?
2. What is your time frame?

These questions have an important interrelationship. What kind of predator are you? Knowing what kind of predator you are is very important because the market is a food chain. In this food chain, various predators are waiting to ambush you and devour your capital. In order to develop the appropriate strategy, you must know your enemies and how they think.

Short-term trading is divided into three different styles: *day trading, microtrend trading,* and *position trend trading.* One reason that short-term traders have such a high percentage of losses is that they are trained to use a standard one-size-fits-all approach. Usually, the entire focus of this approach is to follow short-term momentum and order flow represented by the ticker. This type of trading is referred to as *scalping.* There are two fundamental problems with this approach. First, time and sales are usually late, which no one addresses, and second, individuals are not all the same. Your trading strategy needs to be tailored to your trading ability. What works for someone else won't necessarily work for you. Another reason for failure is that short-term traders, especially day traders, aren't usually trained to screen for high-probability, high-profitability trades. I am going to introduce you to seven short-term trading strategies that are extremely successful. With seven strategies to choose from, it is up to you to select those that fit your needs and apply them. This leads us back to my first question. What kind of predator are you? You have to determine what kind of trader you are. Let's define the three types of short-term traders so that we all understand specifically what we are talking about.

1. *Day trader:* A day trader by our definition is a trader who enters the market at some point during the day and is totally in cash (flat) by the end of the day. At no time does a day trader carry a position overnight. Some day traders trade for fractions of a point—usually $\frac{1}{16}$, $\frac{1}{8}$. This is called *scalping.* This type of day trading has a high failure rate. One out of a hundred thousand people can consistently make money by scalping. You always hear about the exceptions, don't you? The small profit per trade, commissions, slippage, and the possibility of a series of losing trades, make scalping a technique that may not be for you. You may be the exception, but don't lose all your money trying to prove it. Not all day traders are scalpers. For example, *intraday trend traders* will stay in a trade until the trend reverses. This could take a few minutes or several hours. Both types of day traders typically buy 500 to a 1,000 shares or more at a time and must be highly capitalized. The *minimum* day trading capital for an individual trader is usually $50,000 to $100,000. Day trading requires large amounts of operating capital. Most day traders trade several times a day. It's not unusual for a scalper to make 30 to 150 trades or more per day, while the intraday trend traders will make 3 to 9 trades per day.

2. *Microtrend trader:* A microtrend trader by our definition is a trader who takes a position with the intention of holding it for three to five days. The microtrend trader is attempting to trade a small part of a larger trend. A day trader never carries a position overnight, but the microtrend trader does. Usually a stop is strategically placed at the end of day to take the trader out if the trend dramatically reverses. For microtrend trading to be successful the entry must be made when the trend is strong. This usually occurs when the trend is under way or begins explosively. The momentum should carry the price for three to five days. Unlike the day trader who trades for fractions, the microtrend trader typically trades for points. After three to five days, the microtrend trader liquidates his or her position and looks for another microtrend. The *minimum* trading capital for an individual microtrend trader is usually $30,000. Most microtrend traders are very well capitalized, with trading accounts of $100,000 or more. The psychological stress on the microtrend trader is, in most cases, far less than on a day trader, because time is more an ally than an enemy.

3. *Position trend trader:* A position trader attempts to ride the trend for 10 to 14 days or longer. A position trader usually takes a position of *size* (large number of shares) and holds until another position becomes more promising. If a trend is intact, the position trader will roll up stops until the market takes them out. The intention is to stay in the position for 10 to 14 days, but if the trend continues, the position trader will stay with the trend as long as possible. In many cases, a microtrend trader can become a position trend trader if the three- to five-day holding-period trend explodes, carrying prices further. Because position traders are in a trade for a longer period of time, they must allow for price volatility and intelligent stop placement. The minimum trading capital for a position trader varies. If you hold a position beyond one month, you are considered an investor. According to this definition, most fund managers are position traders. In many cases, institutional position traders will add to their positions if they feel the long-term outlook for the stock is positive. Position traders usually move the market because of the collective size of their accumulation (buying) or distribution (selling).

What is your time frame? It should become obvious that understanding your time frame is critical to everything you do in trading. Your trading strategy, application of technical indicators, entry and exit, and so on, are determined by your individual time frame. As a professional who trains individuals to trade, one of the most amazing things I hear when I ask "What is your time frame?" is "I don't know." The very definition of what kind of trader you are is dependent on your concept of time as it relates to trading. Time can be your friend or your enemy, and nothing makes the case clearer than day trading. Each tick in real time, positive or negative, amplifies stresses that exist in your mind. Everything is magnified, and each moment becomes urgent. Decisions have to be made on a second-by-second basis, and as each second passes, another agonizing decision to buy, sell, or hold must be made. At the end of the day, you feel as though you just completed a marathon. Mentally and physically exhausted, you know that tomorrow you must run this marathon again. Obviously, not everyone will succeed as a day trader. This is proven by the failure rate of individuals who attempt to day trade. Many would-be day traders fail because the wrong trading strategy and methodology causes them to overtrade. Many day traders are, in fact, gamblers and can't stop trading. Success in day trading will come when you learn to effectively slow down time. This is accomplished by making fewer trades and selecting those with a higher probability of success and a positive reward-to-risk ratio. In Chapter 3 you will be introduced to various trading strategies. These strategies put time on your side making it far less likely that you will become a market statistic. Before you begin to trade with real money, you absolutely need to define your time frame.

Which Dream Is Right for You?

Are you a day trader, a microtrend trader, or a position trader? Ultimately, you have to make the decision. Don't let your decision be influenced by greed or the input of others. Your decision should be based on your individual psychology, knowledge, trading capital, and so on. Bill began living his dream when he realized that scalping was not for him. Today Bill is very successful as a microtrend trader and position trader and is making a very comfortable living from trading. Some individuals have the psychological makeup necessary to be successful as day traders, while others will be more successful as position traders or microtrend traders. Remember the old saying, "If the shoe fits wear it," and be aware that one size does not fit all.

In the following chapters, I am going to guide you to new awareness and knowledge. Within these pages, many of you will find the answers you need to improve your short-term trading.

chapter 2

electronic trading

The term *online trading* is often misused and abused by the media, professionals, and the public to refer to electronic trading. Let me make this perfectly clear once and for all. Trading online over the Internet and sending orders to an online broker do *not* constitute electronic trading. The two are as different as night and day. If you are trading online, before you can key in your buy or sell order, the electronic trader has already made the trade and received confirmation. Electronic traders route their buy and sell orders through Electronic Communications Networks (ECNs). The watchword of the electronic trader is *speed,* and speed is something you do not have online. Online trading is for investors, not for traders, and for this reason, do not even attempt to day trade online. Online trading was not designed, nor was it ever intended, for day trading. Day trading online is hazardous to your wealth. Let me walk you through a typical online trading experience.

You opened your new online trading account a week ago and you decide that today you will begin trading online. You turn on your computer, and after the third attempt, you establish a good Internet connection. As the data fills your screen you feel power, excitement, and anticipation. Like a modern-day land shark you look for a trading opportunity. As you look at your charts you spot a possible trade. With the click of your mouse you bring up your order screen. You type in the price, the number of shares you want to buy, and identify your order as a limit order by checking the box. You are just about to hit the order button when you see the price change. Do you change the limit order to a market order? All the while time is ticking by. Finally, you decide to send a limit order, but you have to change the price. You do this and hit the Buy button. This cumbersome process took you over 15 seconds. Now that the order has been sent, it will take another 10 seconds for the online broker to receive and act on it. Two minutes later you see your price trade across the screen. Your confirmations arrive by e-mail or by phone. You wait and wait and wait, only to find out 20 minutes later that your order remains unfilled due to fast market conditions. Feeling frustrated and less empowered than 30 minutes ago, you vow to give it another try. As you watch your screen, another opportunity shows itself, and this time you send it as a market order. Two seconds after you hit the Buy button the stock runs up. Online traders do not have the ability to cancel their orders in seconds, with almost instant confirmation, as electronic traders do. Fifteen minutes later you receive an e-mail informing you that you bought the stock at ⅜ of a point higher than when you entered the order, and you decide to sell. You quickly enter another market order, only to find out your order was filled ¼ point lower. That afternoon the mail arrives with your new account information, and the front of the envelope says it all: "Welcome to Online Trading."

This example is not an exaggeration. Online trading lacks the speed and technical sophistication necessary to successfully trade intraday. It is possible to microtrend trade or invest online—but *not* to day trade. Day trading is difficult enough as it is without handicapping yourself by trying to trade online.

Electronic Trading for a Living

I am a professional trader. By that I mean that I make my living *trading* and *training* other professionals and individuals to trade the market. People pay me to help improve their trading skills. If I am successful and improve their ability by a small degree, it could translate into hundreds of thousands of dollars for them. I have found that part of successful trading is knowing the difference between *tools* and *toys* and paying the price for professional results. Let me explain what I mean with a story.

I was in my father's garage returning tools I had borrowed. My father asked me if the tools had been right for the job. I replied, "Yes, they were." He then asked me, "Did you take care of my tools?" Before I could answer, he proceeded to tell me a story, as Texans often do. He said, "When I was young I worked for a man who had a landscaping company. I had just returned from doing a job and was putting away the tools when he asked me, 'Did you take care of my tools?' " Dad said yes. The man said, "I make my living with these tools. Always remember, if you take care of your tools, your tools will take care of you. They make the work I do easier and are worth the price because the best is never cheap. Never buy a toy unless you just want to play." Successful traders use the best tools money can buy because toys will not get professional results. Remember, your competition does not use toys. They play the serious game of taking other people's money: It's called *trading*.

Computerized electronic trading puts you on a level with the professionals. When your order is entered, it is treated just as an order from any major firm. Using this sophisticated technology combined with self-discipline, knowledge, experience, and skill, you have an opportunity to succeed where many others fail. Part of your success will come from an understanding of the various segments that make electronic trading unique to online trading.

Electronic Communications Networks (ECNs)

What are Electronic Communications Networks (ECNs)? Electronic Communications Networks are conduits over which you announce your intentions to buy or sell a stock. Your orders are matched with other orders from individuals like yourself. ECNs add liquidity to the National Association of Securities Dealers Automated Quotations (Nasdaq) system without the involvement of a market maker.

Market makers make their money by creating a spread on each trade. By placing your order on an ECN, in most cases you bypass the spread, because most ECNs do not sell their order flow. I think of ECNs as an electronic dating service for stocks, matching willing buyers with willing sellers.

The broker-dealers subscribe to the ECNs and pay a fee to facilitate the trade. ECNs must be registered with the Nasdaq to participate in the market. The ECN system brings additional customer orders into the Nasdaq market. Both customer orders and market makers post their orders on ECNs to achieve a more liquid market. Electronic trading has been credited with narrowing the spread on most stocks traded on the Nasdaq market. An advantage of electronic trading that is not available to the online trader is the ability to buy on the bid and sell on the ask. Most of the time an online trader sees only the national best bid or offer (NBBO). The electronic trader often splits the bid and offer, thereby narrowing the spread on the stock. Electronic trading tactics will be covered in Chapter 6.

The first ECN, known as *Instinet,* came into existence in 1969. For many years Instinet-owned Reuters was the only ECN around. Today nine ECNs exist and several more are planned for the future. Before I address the different ECNs, I think it is important to note the effect ECNs have had on the New York Stock Exchange (NYSE). Proposed extended trading hours for the NYSE have been the result of pressure put on NYSE by the ECNs. After-hours trading, using ECNs, is forcing the NYSE to make changes in the old way of doing business. In my opinion, the ECNs will bring about 24-hour trading. Not long after that will come global electronic trading for individuals who wish to trade international markets.

Meet the ECNs

As I write this book, there are nine ECNs that are active on a Nasdaq Level II screen. Each ECN is identified by its specific symbol, as are the market makers. Fidelity, Schwab, Donaldson, Lufkin & Jenrette, and Spear, Leeds & Kellogg plan to introduce yet another ECN in late 1999. This ECN could serve as the first after-hours trading platform with substantial liquidity that is accessible to the retail public. Charles Schwab's customer survey indicates that 40 percent of customers who currently give Schwab after-hour orders will trade extended hours. This system will offer the client the ability to trade NYSE stocks as well as stocks traded on the Nasdaq. As you can see, the ECNs are going to bring about more change in the next five years than has transpired in the past hundred years. Even the way the industry does business will be forever altered. Let me briefly introduce you to the current ECNs.

Instinet (INCA)

The ECN Instinet was originally designed to make markets between institutions. Today you can access the Instinet ECN if your broker dealer has an arrangement allowing you to do so. Not all electronic trading firms are created equal. You will find that some firms do not allow you to use certain ECNs; this is a business decision of each particular firm. Instinet allows you to trade 45 minutes before and after NYSE hours. Instinet is not considered a retail ECN, as most of its activity is institutional trading.

Island (ISLD)

Island is the most liquid of the retail ECNs. Island has had days when trading volume was greater than on Instinet. This is partly due to the fact the institutional traders were hiding orders on Island and did not want to post them on Instinet. In this way they can mask their size (number of shares) and intentions. Like most ECNs, Island is new, coming into existence in 1996. In a small amount of time it has become one of the most active ECNs. Island allows you to enter only *limit* orders, and because you can not specify *all-or-none* orders, you may receive a partial fill. For example, you wanted to sell 1,000 shares but were filled with only 500. Island will many times fill you in *odd lots* (uneven number of shares). To avoid a partial fill, make sure that your order reflects the *size* (number of shares) posted at the bid and ask on the Level II screen. These posted bids and offers (ask) represent the best bids and offers and are posted on the Nasdaq Level II screen. When you route an order to ISLD, it is posted into what is called the *Island book*. This book lists all buy and sell orders. Any buy or sell orders that arrive simultaneously and are the same price are executed instantly. If you place a buy or sell order on Island and currently there is no market at your price, the order will *sit* on the book until it can be matched with another order. Whenever you see an Island order posted on the Level II screen, you are trading against another Island trader. Island will be one of the most used and liquid ECNs. Island has extended its trading hours in preparation for 24-hour trading.

Archipelago (ARCA, TNTO, ARCHIP)

Many electronic day trading firms do not have access to ECN Archipelago. As is the case with all ECNs, the broker-dealer must subscribe. In some cases, these broker-dealer firms do not subscribe to ARCA. This can be a disadvantage to a trader unless he or she has a way to get around the problem of not being able to use certain ECNs in specific situations (see Chapter 5). Again, not all electronic trading firms are equal.

The ECN Archipelago has advantages and disadvantages. Let us examine the advantages first. Suppose you have stock you want to sell on the bid side. Archipelago acts like a *bot* (computer sequenced automatic robot program) and will seek out the market maker on the bid. It poles the market maker, and if that market maker cannot fill the order, it moves to the next most active market maker right down the line. Archipelago will also go to the ECNs to complete your order command. Archipelago will hit market makers and ECNs to complete your order. If Archipelago cannot match the order on its own book, it will send it to the national market, which connects to Island, Instinet, and SelectNet. This means an order that would normally be rejected (i.e., would sit in the book) is executed as fast as possible. Archipelago will also fill you in round lots, and Archipelago is easy to use. For example, if you want to join either the bid or the ask, you simply enter your price on the bid when buying and on the ask when selling. Another advantage of Archipelago is that when ECNs like BRUD or REDI are stopping the market, you can hit them. Electronic firms that do not subscribe to Archipelago may not be able to hit them. If you are on the bid or the ask, you can be hit only by someone who preferences you; this can be an advantage.

One would think that an ECN that worked until your order was filled would be very advantageous, but the mechanics that allow Archipelago to perform this task are also disadvantageous. Let's now look at the disadvantages of Archipelago. When Archipelago goes to the market maker to fill the order, it uses what is called a SelectNet preference to show orders to the market makers. The market maker has 20 seconds to accept the offer. This 20-second period is a major disadvantage because a lot can happen in those 20 seconds. If the order is not completely filled, it will keep on trying to fill it until the order is totally complete. The problem is that the buyer takes the number of shares he or she wants. Chapters 5 and 6 show specific examples of how to use the Archipelago ENC when routing under specific conditions.

Currently, about one-third of the volume on Archipelago is generated by broker-dealers trading their own accounts, a third by institutions, and the rest by private customers of broker-dealers and individual traders.

Attain (ATTN)

The ECN symbol ATTN was launched in February of 1998. If the broker-dealer is a subscriber to the ATTN, ECN traders may match orders to the ATTN book. Nonsubscribers can use SelectNet to preference the ATTN ECN. Attain's primary focus is the retail day trader. The volume of activity on the ATTN ECN is low compared to other ECNs. Even though this ECN caters to day traders, the activity does not compare to Island or Archipelago.

Brut (BRUT)

Most users of the BRUT ECN are members of Brokerage Real-Time Applications System Software (BRASS). If your broker-dealer has a subscription to Archipelago, you can hit the ECN BRUT.

Redibook (REDI)

Spear, Leeds & Kellogg created this ECN to support a proprietary interface called REDIPlus. REDI is an active participant in the market and currently targets professional traders and institutional investors.

Strike (STRK)

The Strike ECN is available to post bids and offers. It has a different business model. The broker-dealers pay only when they use it.

Bloomberg B-Trade (BTRD)

The ECN BTRD is an active participant in the market and, along with REDI, has large-volume activity.

NexTrade (NEXT)

NexTrade is the first ECN to provide 24-hour electronic order execution to retail traders. NexTrade allows its customers anonymity to enter and exit a market. You are able to place Nasdaq and NYSE limit orders.

Currently ECNs are used to trade stocks on the Nasadaq system and can be viewed on a Nasdaq Level II screen. Level II screens will be discussed later in this chapter, along with price tickers and order routing.

Who Owns the ECNs

ECN	*Owner*
Instinet	Reuters
Island	Datek On-line
Archipelago	E-Trade; Goldman Sachs; Townsend Analytics; TerraNova; Southwest Securities
Attain	All-Tech Investments (day trading firm)
Brut	SunGard; Merrill Lynch; Morgan Stanley; Dean Witter; Goldman Sachs; Knight Trimark
Redibook	Spear, Leeds & Kellogg
Strike	Bear Stearns; Lehman Brothers; J.P. Morgan; Donaldson, Lufkin & Jenrette; Salomon Smith Barney; Bridge Data; Herzog, Heine, Geduld; Sun Microsystems
B-Trade	Bloomberg
NexTrade	Pim Global Equities
Name Unknown	Fidelity Investments; Charles Schwab; Donaldson, Lufkin & Jenrette; Spear, Leeds & Kellogg

Let us continue our look at mechanisms for trading the Nasdaq market. Later we will cover trading stocks listed on the NYSE using the Super DOT system.

Small Order Execution System (SOES)

The public, which includes online Internet traders, always buys high on the *ask* and sells low on the *bid,* hoping the stock will move higher. Market makers and professional traders always have had the advantage of buying low and selling high. SOES is an electronic trading system that is designed to execute public market and limit orders. I use the term *public* because SOES cannot be used by institutions to trade their own in-house accounts. If you use the SOES system, you can buy ✓ on the bid and sell on the ask. This is because the market makers must fill the *first* electronic pulse that hits their best bid or ask price. This is known as the *inside market.* The speed of execution on these orders is measured in seconds. It is mandatory for all registered market makers to honor SOES orders. Since they are willing to buy and sell on both sides of a market in a given stock, they have to post *size* (number of shares) for the bid and the ask. The correct terminology for this is *tier* size. It ranges between 200, 500, and 1,000 shares. At this point, the market maker begins to play a little game with you, called "truth or lie." You have to figure out if the market maker is posting his or her required tier size or if the market maker is a net seller or buyer of the stock. One thing for sure, the market makers will try to hide their true intentions as long as possible.

The largest number of shares you can buy or sell on the SOES system is 1,000 shares. There have been discussions of increasing the number of shares you may buy on the SOES system, but as of now, 1,000 is the maximum.

SOES routing is the second most useful tool for traders who want high-speed execution when buying and selling. SOES does, however, have some restrictions that must be considered when you are routing your trades through the system. Because market makers must maintain both sides of the market and honor the first electronic pulse (order) that hits their bid or offer (ask), SOES has the following rules.

The Rules of Engagement: When You Trade SOES, It's War

SOES has what is known as the *five-minute rule.* If you buy, for example, 1,000 shares of stock, you have to wait five minutes to buy

again on the SOES system. This in my opinion is the biggest limita-
tion of the SOES system. If you wanted to turn around and sell that
same 1,000 shares you could, but after you do, you will have to wait
another five minutes to sell. The five-minute rule applies to the buy
and the sell. If you forget and try to sell or buy when the five-minute
rule is in force, the system will cancel your order. About now you
are saying to yourself, "Forget it, this SOES stuff is a pain in the
assets." Do not worry, I have the answer for you. In the previous
paragraph I said, "SOES routing is the *second* most useful tool for
traders who want high-speed execution when buying and selling."
The *first* is Island. You can use the ECN Island to get around the
SOES five-minute rule. For example, you buy 500 shares on the
SOES system, and a minute later you want to buy 500 more. To
accomplish this you route a buy order over Island for 500 shares,
and presto, you are filled. Island has no restrictions on size or time
execution. You can then sell 1,000 shares on SOES or use the ECN
Island (ISLD).

I live in the San Gabriel mountains overlooking Los Angles. If
you look into the distant night sky, you will see a string of beautiful lights. These lights are large commercial passenger jets on a
flight path to land at Los Angeles International Airport. They line
up for over 300 miles on their approach to Los Angeles International. Keep this image in your mind as we address another SOES
problem.

You are one trader among thousands using the SOES system.
You are all using the same system to place your buy and sell orders.
Remember, market makers are on both sides of the market, and
they are required to fill the first electronic pulse that hits the inside
market. If your pulse is not the first, you are filled in the order
received. In other words, you line up and take your turn to land on
the bid or the ask. This leads to partial fills. If your order is not executed by the first market maker, the SOES system will seek out the
next market maker and place you in line. Just as in grade school,
you can get into trouble while waiting in line. If you place a SOES
limit order and the market maker *lifts* the offer, your order is canceled. Chapter 5 offers an example of using a SOES limit order in
shorting stock.

Seventeen seconds can feel like an eternity when you just hit the bid and nothing happens. *Hit the bid* means that you just sold stock at the current bid price if the market maker is in what is called a *refresh*. Market makers have 17 seconds once they have filled their SOES obligation to decide to stay with the price or change the price. Just when you thought it could not get any worse, it did. Market makers have access to Nasdaq Level III information. This tells them where and how many buyers and sellers are gathering. They also have access to what is known as *SOES buster* software. This enables the market makers to shake out the day trading scalpers who typically trade for ⅟₁₆ and ⅛ of a point.

Even though SOES has some definite disadvantages, its speed and reliability makes it one of the short-term traders' preferred routing systems. To put all of this in prospective, sing the following to the tune of Kenny Rodgers song "The Gambler."

> You got to know when to hold 'em, know when to SOES 'em, know when to hit the bid and sell on the ask. You never count your money when sitting on the open. . . . There will be time enough for counting when the trading's done.

SelectNet

In reality, SelectNet is an order-routing system that allows negotiation. Remember, Archipelago uses a SelectNet preference that gives market makers 20 seconds to decide if they want to accept the order or reject it. This negotiation is between market markers. One way of using the SelectNet preference would be to place an order on Archipelago to find a price that is better than the current advertised price. This might happen if a short seller needs stock to cover a short squeeze and is willing to pay ⅛ more than the current price near the close of the day. SelectNet has no time or size limits.

Nasdaq Routing

You know about the various ECNs, SOES, and SelectNet. The question you might be asking about now is, "Which one of these do I route my order through." Three offer the speed and liquidity that intraday traders and microtrend traders need.

1. Island (LSLD)

2. Small Order Execution System (SOES)

3. Archipelago (ARCA, TNTO, ARCHIP)

Super DOT: Trading with the Big Boys

Tremendous opportunity exists in trading large-cap stocks on the New York Stock Exchange (NYSE). Most of the time, when you hear the term *electronic trading* you think about using the ECNs and trading the Nasdaq market. You can trade the NYSE electronically by accessing the Super DOT system. If your electronic brokerage firm has an affiliate-member relationship that enables it to route orders to the floor, you can trade the NYSE electronically. If it does not, you will not be able to trade the NYSE. In some cases, day trading firms do not allow traders access to the NYSE or AMEX markets because of costs associated with doing so. These firms prefer to trade only Nasdaq stocks. The NYSE and the AMEX markets can be traded using the Super DOT (Super Designated Order Turnaround) system. This system allows traders to place orders that are routed to the appropriate specialist or member brokerage post on the floor. Super DOT usually carries smaller orders; however, this system is responsible for over half the orders traded on the NYSE. To a great extent, the Super DOT system enables program trading. Armed with this information and using your imagination, you should see an advantage that, with a little work, could give you an edge over other traders who see only the obvious.

In my opinion, not being able to trade the NYSE and AMEX electronically is a great disadvantage. When looking for an electronic trading firm, make sure that it offers you the ability to route your order through ECNs, SOES, and the Super DOT system. You want flexibility in routing because this translates into an advantage over those who do not have it. All three options (ECNs, SOES, Super DOT) give you the power to route the trade appropriately.

The major difference in trading the NYSE versus the Nasdaq is that the NYSE is an auction market, and specialists maintain and make orderly markets. They stand ready to provide liquidity. This is a tall order given the size and volatility of the markets. To expedite the process, the specialist is given latitude in decision making. A good example of this, and one you can profit from, is when a specialist has been given a very large order (size) to buy. If you have a *limit order or better order* sitting in place to *sell,* you have a very good chance of getting a higher price. If the specialist needs to buy within a price range and does not have the time necessary to fill the order in small blocks, you are the winner. The same would be true if the specialist had a large order (size) to sell. If your *buy* limit order is sitting at the right price in the book, you could be filled at a lower price. I have had this happen to me numerous times, and I always look at it as a bonus for trading the NYSE or AMEX markets. Getting a better price on the buy and sell is known as *price improvement.* The Pacific Stock Exchange, for example, prides itself on making an orderly market and has an excellent record for price improvement. Whenever I can, I let them, and other exchanges, help me as much as possible.

Sometimes, traders who exclusively trade the Nasdaq electronically exhibit some rather peculiar behavior. I particularly enjoy one I call *hyperdrive.* After about three months of trading, otherwise calm, relaxed individuals go through a transformation. They seem to live in a reality where events are moving at the speed of light, and they move right along with them. They are in a hurry to get to wherever it is they are going, and once they get there, they are in a hurry to leave. They talk fast, walk fast, and if you are moving too slowly they will quickly let you know. One day at tradingschool.com I was leading a training session on the Super DOT system. In the class was a trader who had traded only the Nasdaq and wanted to learn about Super DOT. A trader who is trading electronically in most cases will be able to buy or sell in two seconds or less, which includes the confirmation—very fast indeed. When you use the Super DOT system, it could take 3 to 12 seconds, and in rare cases longer. I would estimate that the average time for a trade using the Super DOT is somewhere around three to six seconds. Mr. Nasdaq clicked the buy button and the trade went in on Super DOT;

it took four seconds. Mr. Nasdaq's comment was, "Seems a little slow to me." Fifteen minutes later I watched as he entered a buy limit order, and this time it took seven seconds. As I watched him during that seven seconds, his facial expressions would have led you to think he was having some kind of seizure. He was in agony waiting, and those five extra seconds seemed to him like an eternity. When the trade posted on the real-time blotter, he gave a sigh of relief that could be heard across the room. At the end of the day he said, "How can you stand waiting that long?" I laughed and said, "The trade took a total of only seven seconds and you had price improvement on the trade. I think that is worth waiting for." If five extra seconds drives *you* crazy with stress, maybe you shouldn't be trading. *Hyperdrive* behavior is a symptom of emotional trading that may lead to gambling behavior. A little stress is normal, but if you become stressed over a five-second time period, you had better take a look at your behavior. I will continue to use the Super DOT system, enduring the extra five seconds and the possibility of price improvement while laughing all the way to the bank. We will look at a few examples of trading using the Super DOT system in Chapter 6.

Trading the NYSE or AMEX using the Super DOT system can be very profitable. The lack of volatility is made up by the stock's high-probability behavior. Contrary to popular momentum dogma, a stock with *personality* (a degree of predictable behavior) is far more desirable than one with volatility. I would rather make several high-probability trades than to roll the dice on Internet stocks and try to hit home runs all the time. While Nasdaq stocks certainly have high-probability trading opportunities, the NYSE is not typically a hotbed of speculation. Mindless volatility should be avoided at all costs because it usually does not translate into trend. If you think for one minute that you are always going to be on the right side of volatility, think again. Traders use a term known as the *stick*. The stick is a price bar that could be intraday, daily, weekly, or monthly. If you are one who seeks out the most volatile stocks without looking at probability, you are going to take a beating with the volatility stick, and I can assure you it is going to hurt. Do not trade the Nasdaq or the NYSE unless your focus is high-probability trading.

Nasdaq Market Makers

The Nasdaq market is made up of over 500 market makers and ECNs, all of whom are attempting to improve liquidity. The market makers are divided into two groups. One is made up of *institutional* market makers, such as Goldman Sachs, and the rest fall into what I term *retail* market makers. Both are required to maintain liquidity on both sides of the market. If market makers are willing to sell a stock at a set price, they must be willing to buy it back. When you buy or sell a stock on the Nasdaq, you need to understand that the same market maker who sold you stock at a certain price is more than willing to buy it back from you at a lower price. Market makers always buy low and sell high. Market makers' willingness to buy and sell at specific prices is reflected on a Nasdaq Level II screen. They literally advertise their intention to either buy or sell. Just as a specialist is assigned specific stocks on the NYSE, the Nasdaq market makers are responsible for providing liquidity for a group of stocks. In most cases, the stocks for which they make markets have varying degrees of volatility. By balancing the volatility, the market makers can perform their function more efficiently. This is not just for the benefit of the public, because, like specialists, market makers can and do trade for their own accounts.

Institutional Market Makers

There is an old riddle that goes, "How do you dance with a 500-pound gorilla?" The answer is, "Any way he wants." When it comes to the markets, one of your jobs is to quickly ascertain which 500-pound gorilla is trading the stock. The major player in the stock is known as the *ax* because if you are not paying attention to what this player is doing, you may lose you head and your money. The ax is more prominent in stocks that are not heavily traded. In that case, you need to follow what the ax is doing very carefully. A stock like Microsoft that has enormous trading volume makes it difficult, if not impossible, for one market maker to dominate trading in that stock. You will see three or more market makers who are active on any given day in a stock like Microsoft. Again, you need to know what the market markers are doing. Are they buying and selling at a specific price level? Are they buying and selling for their own account or their customer accounts? If they are buying for their own accounts, they want to buy low and sell high. This means that they are buying stock on the bid and offering stock on the ask. In general, market makers buy stocks that are going down and sell stocks that are going up. They do this in small fractions of a point, which makes market markers the *ultimate scalpers.* Institutional market makers represent their customers (i.e., other firms or their retail account clients) or themselves. When they represent themselves, they are trading for their own accounts and tend to be out of the trade very quickly. When they represent the client, they are acting in an agent capacity and receive a commission. These trades are in most cases positions of longer time frames and are typically large numbers of shares. You want to identify the institutional market makers because they carry the big *stick,* and if you are not on the right side of the trend they can beat you with it. Following are lists of institutional market makers and retail market makers, along with their symbols. The market makers that make a market in a specific stock are displayed on a Nasdaq Level II screen. A few market makers (e.g., Merrill Lynch) are both institutional and retail market makers. A good example of a retail market maker would be Dean Witter or Charles Schwab. These market makers buy and sell in an agent capacity, thus providing liquidity for the market.

Retail Market Makers		*Institutional Market Makers*	
Bear Sterns	BEST	Cowen & Co.	COWN
Herzog, Heine, Geduld	HRZG	Credit Suisse/First Boston	FBCO
Mayer Schweitzer	MASH	Goldman Sachs	GSCO
Montgomery Securities	MONT	Merrill Lynch	MLCO
Nash Weiss & Co	NAWE	Salomon Smith Barney	SBSH
Olde Discount	OLDE		
Sherwood Securities	SHWD		

You want to make note of who is on the bid or ask. Are the retail market makers selling customer orders, or are the institutional market makers buying or selling for their own account?

The following is a more extensive list of market makers. Those shown are the major market makers. (The list is not complete as there are more than 500 market makers.)

Market Makers List

Alex Brown	BTSC
Bear Sterns*	BEST
CIBC Oppenheimer*	OPCO
Cowen & Co.	COWN
Credit Suisse/First Boston*	FBCO
Dean Witter Reynolds Inc.*	DEAN
Donaldson, Lufkin & Jenrette*	DLJP
Goldman Sachs[†]	GSCO
Gruntal & Co.	GRUN
Herzog, Heine, Geduld[†]	HRZG
Jefferies & Co.	JEFF
J.P. Morgan Securities[†]	JPMS
Knight Securities LP[†]	NITE
Lehman Brothers*	LEHM
Mayer Schweitzer[†]	MASH
Merrill Lynch[†]	MLCO
Montgomery Securities*	MONT
Morgan Stanley[†]	MSCO
Nash Weiss & Co.	NAWE
Needham & Co.*	NEED
PaineWebber[†]	PWJC
Prudential Securities*	PRUS
Robert Stephens	RSSF
Salomon Smith Barney[†]	SBSH
Schonfeld Securities	SHON
Soundview Financial	SNDV
Togster Singer Corp.	TSCO
Tucker Anthony	TUCK
UBS Securities	UBSS

* Indicates major market makers.
[†] Indicates that the market maker is the ax on many occasions.

There are many additional market makers, but the ones listed here seem to be the most active, becoming the *ax* in a given market (i.e., the major buyer or seller who makes the market around which everyone else participates).

Nasdaq Level II Screens

The market maker screens show the depth of the market in a specific stock and the participants within that market. When you look at a Nasdaq Level II market maker screen you see the market makers and the ECNs who make up that market. Trying to trade without Level II capability is like trying to fly a plane without instruments. The Nasdaq Level II screen shows you information you need to trade successfully. Level II is also useful for trading the NYSE and the AMEX. While those exchanges do not show the same information as the Nasdaq, they do show various expressions of interest. Knowing what to look for in the Level II screens is important to short-term entry and exit strategy. Remember, market makers, who are professionals and must provide liquidity on both sides of the market, are the ones you are competing against. Never forget that you are up against professionals who in most cases have more knowledge, experience, and capital than you do. Remembering this will keep you humble when you have a series of winning trades. Controlling the euphoria of winning will keep you from giving back all your profit. Trade from the *alpha zone* (you will learn about this state of mind in Chapter 7), not with your ego or emotion.

Five years ago the market maker screens were far more useful for entry and exit strategy than they are in the present. When Nasdaq Level II technology and order routing through ECNs were new, spreads on stocks were much wider than they are today. As this technology became increasingly available and more traders began to trade more extensively, the spreads began to shrink. Market makers are now using the Level II screens to lure day traders who scalp into deadly traps. Using Level III and SOES buster software, which charts the movements of day traders, they bait the trap. Armed with this information they spring the trap and use the electronic day trader's own knowledge of trading to *their advantage*. Compounding this problem further, most day trading firms that train traders to scalp have not addressed the changes in reading the Level II screen. The market is a dynamic place, and change is the rule, not the exception. If your information is outdated and your opponent is using it against you, what chance of success do you think you have? Your competition will spend time and money to stay informed and ahead of the learning curve, and so must you. The first one to the dinner table gets the most food. The last gets whatever is left. If you are not informed, you may be the main course. Remember that the market is a food chain.

Level II market maker information is usually associated with the Nasdaq market and the stocks that trade there. You can use the Level II screens on the NYSE and the AMEX markets to see the level of interest in a specific stock. Of course, the depth of information is not even close to that of the Nasdaq market, but you can see the bid, ask, and size of all six exchanges. This is certainly better than looking at one bid and ask on the stock. Let us take a look at the mechanical components of a Nasdaq Level II market maker screen of the Nasdaq and the NYSE (see Figures 2.1 and 2.2). We can also

Figure 2.1   Nasdaq Level II market maker box
Used with permission of Townsend Analytics, Ltd.

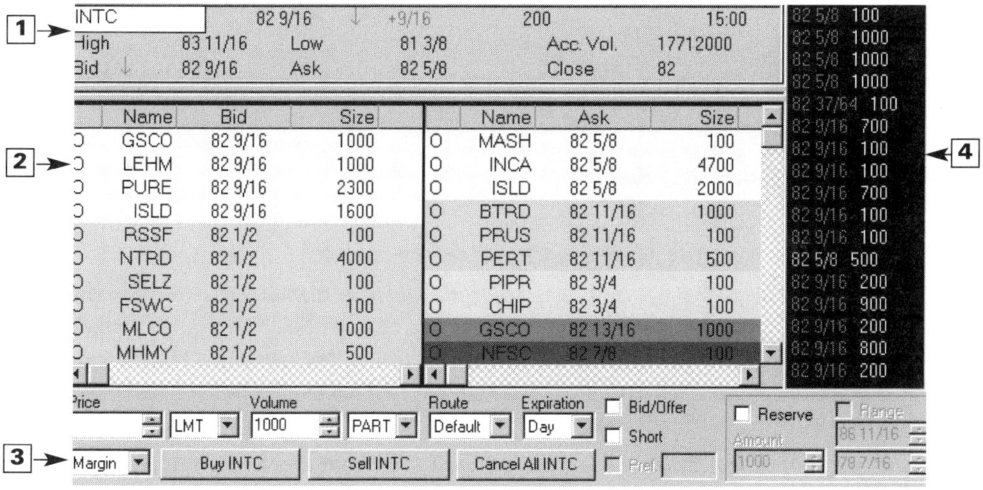

1. This area shows the active information (high, low, close, time, volume, etc.).

2. This part of the Level II screen shows the bid and ask (offer) side of the market. *You will see both ECNs and market makers.* You can see the size and the various orders

making up this market. *Remember, this size is only what they want you to see.* This is much better than seeing just the active market that most people see.

3. This section shows the order-entry and -routing box from which you buy, sell, cancel orders, or go short. You can enter your price, the number of shares, and, most important, the route your order will take: ISLD, ARCA, SOES, or DOT. This part of the trading configuration is the most powerful; you can place a trade and get a fill, in most cases, in a few seconds.

4. This vertical color-coded ticker shows the size of the trade. Green is buying and red is selling.

Figure 2.2 Market maker box on NYSE
Used with permission of Townsend Analytics, Ltd.

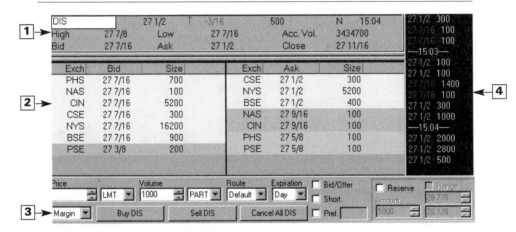

1. Here you see the active information (high, low, volume, etc.) for the Level II screen.

2. This part shows the bid and ask (offer) side of the market and the different exchanges. Because this stock is on the NYSE, the screen doesn't show the different market makers. You can see the size and the various orders making up this market. This is much better than seeing just the national best bid or offer (NBBO) that most people see.

3. This section shows the order-entry and -routing box from which you buy, sell, cancel orders, or go short. This part of the trading configuration is the most powerful because you can place a trade and get a fill in seconds. Using the Super DOT will take longer than using ECNs or SOES.

4. This vertical color-coded ticker shows the size of the trade. Green is buying and red is selling.

examine the order-routing box and the price ticker. All of this information is important to your decision-making process.

Figure 2.3 shows a more complete explanation of a Nasdaq Level II market maker screen with ticker and order-routing box.

The ticker shows the time of a trade, the number of shares, and the price (see Figure 2.4). In the past, too much emphasis has been

Figure 2.3   Nasdaq market maker screen
Used with permission of Townsend Analytics, Ltd.

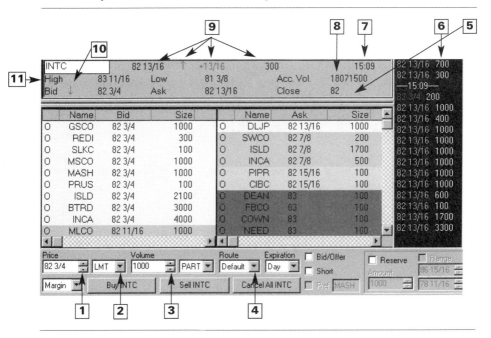

1. *Price box:* There are two ways of entering a price into the price box. The first is to simply place the pointer at any price you select on the bid or the ask side of the screen and click the mouse. The price will appear in the price box. If you want to raise or lower the price by fractions of a point you can use the up and down buttons located to the right of the box. This enables you to make small adjustments to the price very quickly. The second way of entering the price is to use the computer keyboard and type in the price.

2. *Order type:* This box is used to identify your order by clicking on the arrow at the far right of the box. When you click on the arrow you will be able to select a limit order or a market order.

3. *Number of shares:* Enter the number of shares by typing the number into the space available. You can make changes by using the increase and decrease button at the right.

4. *Route:* Use this button to select the various options available to route your order. Make sure the correct route is selected before you make the trade.

5. *Yesterday's close:* This information can give you a point of reference during the trading day.

6. *Ticker:* The ticker shows the most recent trade and the size of the order. The ticker can be color-coded and has several configuration options. For example, you can set it to show trades of only 1,000 shares or more.

7. *Time:* This shows the time at that minute in Eastern Standard Time.

8. *Accumulated volume for day:* This shows the total accumulated volume for the day up to that point in time.

9. *Last trade:* The last trade shows the price of the last trade, whether the price is up or down for the day, and the direction of change in price of the last trade price uptick or downtick. The size of the trade is also shown.

10. *Change in bid:* This shows the last change in the bid and whether it was an uptick or a downtick. This information is important because you cannot short a downtick on the bid.

11. *High and low:* The high and low for the day are shown in this area of the Level II market maker box.

Figure 2.4   Price ticker
Used with permission of Townsend Analytics, Ltd.

placed on the ticker and ticker-related information. This information is colored-coded. In most cases, red identifies selling and green buying. A mixed market is an even distribution of both buying and selling. Scalpers use this ticker information in an attempt to make a fraction of a point on the trade. They are taught to watch this information and act on it. The problem with this approach is that you are not really seeing a true picture of what is going on. Time and sales are full of incorrect data. From mistakes to late reporting, the ticker is the last thing you should use to enter and exit trades. There is a way of correcting to some extent the problems with ticker data to make it a more accurate tool for traders. This will be discussed in Chapter 6.

Order-Routing System

In the previous pages you were introduced, by description, to the order-routing box that sits at the bottom of a Nasdaq Level II market maker screen. This is the most important part of your trading configuration. The design and function of this box will depend on your electronic trading firm. As I have stated before, not all electronic brokers are the same. In fact, another individual could be using the same basic software as you, but the look, feel, and function of the screens are different. Software manufacturers make deals with the major electronic trading companies to customize software with their name or a product name. The software is the same, but incorporates the look and function that a particular electronic trading firm wants to offer its clients. Take a very close look at the order-routing system you are offered because the ease and speed of use will in many cases make the difference in getting or missing a trade. You do not want a cumbersome, time-intensive, order-routing system. Another problem with online software is that it simply takes too long to enter the information and route the trade. Let us examine a very powerful order-routing system. Figure 2.5 shows an example of an efficient order-routing system and a brief explanation of the features.

You now have an understanding of the components that make up electronic trading and a clear idea of how much power flexibility this type of trading offers. Once the general public understands how

---

Figure 2.5 Order-routing software
Used with permission of Townsend Analytics, Ltd.

---

1. *Margin:* This area identifies the trade as a margin or cash nonleverage trade.

2. *Price box:* There are two ways of entering a price into the price box. The first is to simply place the pointer on any price you select on the bid or the ask side of the screen and click the mouse. The price will appear in the price box. If you want to raise or lower the price by fractions of a point you can use the up and down buttons located to the right of the box. This enables you to make small adjustments to the price very quickly. The second way of entering price is to use the computer keyboard and type in the price of the trade.

3. *Order type:* This box is used to identify your order by clicking on the arrow at the far right of the box. When you click on the arrow you will be able to select a limit order or a market order. If you are routing using Island, you will want to use the limit identifier. A SOES order may be either limit or market depending on what you are trying to accomplish.

4. *Number of shares:* Enter the number of shares by typing the number into the space available. You can make changes by using the increase and decrease button at the right. Make sure you have selected the correct number of shares before you route the trade. If you want to buy 1,000 shares, you do not want to fire off an order only to see 10,000 in the box. One extra zero is all it takes.

5. *Part or all:* This identifies that all or part of the order must be filled. In most cases you will leave it as part. If you order 500 shares, using part may fill 300, then complete the order with 200.

6. *Route:* The route button selects the route of the trade. By clicking on it you can select from several ways to route your order. This information is critical when momentum increases or decreases. Knowing the correct route will enable you to get out or in on a timely basis. You will be routing to ECNs, SOES, and Super DOT using your member association.

7. *Expiration:* This identifies your order as a day order, good-till-canceled order, or whatever. In most cases you will have the expiration set on a day when you are intraday trading.

8. *Buy button:* This button is used to buy long stock or to cover (buy back) short stock.

9. *Sell button:* This button is used to sell long stock or to short sell.

10. *Cancel button:* This button is used to cancel all orders on the Nasdaq, NYSE, or AMEX. This button is very important to all traders. You need to have the ability to cancel your trades quickly.

---

superior electronic trading is compared to online trading, they will demand it.

Technology is useless without an understanding of how to apply trading strategy. In Chapter 3 we will discuss useful market information and take a look at several trading strategies that can be used by day traders, microtrend traders, and position trend traders.

chapter 3

trading strategies

Trading strategy should fit your personality, time frame, and specific trading style. A combination of the right strategies can enhance and improve most short-term trading results. One factor contributing to the high failure rate for many short-term traders is a one-dimensional trading approach. A multidimensional approach, giving the trader flexibility to adapt to market dynamics, is far more advantageous. Because the market is dynamic, no single strategy will work all the time. If you know only one trading strategy, your days as a successful trader are numbered. Finding the right combination of trading strategies is of the utmost importance to your success. Ultimately, you will decide which combination is best suited for your use. Before we examine various trading strategies, a few other things are critical to your understanding.

The Magic Numbers

Let me ask you an extremely important question. What is the optimum number of trades that exhibit the highest probability of success during a day, week, month, or year on a given security? The answer to this question may profoundly alter the way you currently trade. Traders trade because they want to compound money over the shortest period of time. In many cases, this leads to overtrading, and some traders actually begin to gamble. This is particularly true for *scalpers,* who typically make a large number of trades on any given day. In training day traders who trade electronically, I have found one of the biggest obstacles they need to overcome is their compulsion to overtrade. For some, it's truly an addiction. If not addressed, this addiction can lead to a painful withdrawal from your trading account and ultimately end your life as a trader. You know you have what I term *traders addiction* when you start rationalizing reasons to make trade after trade. When you start finding good reasons to make bad decisions, and when you can't sit at your trading desk without clicking off 30 trades or more, you have traders addiction. The ultimate disaster is trying to trade your way out of a series of losing trades. If you do all of these things, then you are an addict. Traders addiction is exacerbated by trading techniques and strategies that are usually taught by electronic trading firms. Overtrading is *never* in your best interest. Enter a trade only when the probability and profitably is in your favor. Your goal is to find a strategy and a methodology that fit your trading style and benefit you. A good electronic trading firm should care about your success and accommodate you.

What is the optimum number of trades that exhibit the highest profitability and probability of success during a day, week, month, or year on a given security? After years of trading experience and in-depth computer analysis, I have found the answer: *three to five.* These are the *magic numbers* every trader should keep in mind when trading. These magic numbers have a time-cycle correlation associated with them. The first two hours of the trading day and the last two and a half hours are the optimum times for the trader to achieve the highest probability and profitability outcome. *Make only three to five trades per trading vehicle and try to limit your trading to the first two hours and the last two hours of the trading day.* By following this approach you will be making the maximum number of high-probability trades per trading vehicle during those times when market volatility is in your favor and trend is usually obvious. If you trade in the middle of the day, you enter what is known as the *grinder*, whereby you "grind away" most of your morning's profits in increments of ⅛ or ¼ point. Most traders who overtrade are addicted to the action and find themselves in the grinder every day. Don't overtrade, and remember the old adage, "There is a time and a place for everything." Let's take a closer look at the numbers and what they mean for the trader.

The Optimum Maximum Numbers

Only three to five trades will have a reward-to-risk ratio of 2.5 or greater. Using three trades as the more conservative number, we can derive the optimum maximum number of trades per day, week, month, and year. Each trading vehicle should give you three high-probability trades a day; therefore, the maximum number of trades would be three trades times the number of real-time security windows (three), which would equal nine. If you are a day trader, by definition you must be in a cash position at the end of the day. In this example, for you the maximum number of trades would be 18, reflecting the buy and the sell. If you are a day trader and you are exceeding 18 trades a day, in all probability you are *gambling*, not trading. The most profitable short-term traders make no more than three to nine entry trades a day. The optimum maximum number of trades is *nine*. The optimum number of trading vehicles you can monitor successfully at any one time is limited by a human's ability to concentrate and physically react. Time-and-motion studies show that for the majority of people, following more than three positions in real time is nearly impossible.

One Trade at a Time

During the day, while you are monitoring three real-time trading candidates, you are waiting for one of the three to give you the best entry signal. Once you have entered a trade on security A, stay with that trade. If security B gives you a strong entry signal, and it looks like B has more profit potential than A, *exit your first trade* and take the profit. Don't make the mistake of having several positions open at one time. When you are in a trade, you need 100 percent of your focus on that specific trade. You cannot manage more than one trade at a time and react quickly enough to market dynamics. Even though you have computer alerts, and your ego tells you that you can react fast enough, don't do it. One of the most common mistakes I witness traders making is getting greedy and taking multiple positions, thus fragmenting their focus. The worst offender is the trader who enters one position *long* and simultaneously shorts another. Any profit he or she made on one position is canceled out by the loss on the other. If you fragment your focus most of the time, both trades end up losers. Remember, you make money one trade at a time.

How many trades should a high-probability, high-profitability trader consider when using the more conservative approach? How many trades indicate overtrading? Let's take a look at how the answers to these questions impact short-term trading.

Conservative Numbers

Even though you have a potential of three to nine trades a day, that does not mean you have to take every trade. "Every day is not a trading day" from a reward-to-risk standpoint. You want to take the trade that gives you the best signals and the highest profit potential. Some days are obviously better than others. There will be days when you are not at your best physically or emotionally. Despite your desire to trade, do your trading account a favor and don't trade on days when you are not 100 percent ready. *The figures in Table 3.1 make the assumption that you have only three high-probability trades per time cycle, and they reflect only the buy entry.* Looking at the numbers, you can determine that a *day trader* should have 15 high-probability, high-profitability buying trades a week, a

Table 3.1 Conservative trades

	Per Day	Per Week	Per Month	Per Year
Day trader	3	15	60	720
Microtrend trader		3	12	144
Position trader			3	36

microtrend trader 3 trades per week, and a *position trader* 3 trades a month. Compare this to your own trading record and results. If you are exceeding the monthly and annual conservative numbers, you may be pushing your trading, and your results will more than likely reflect that fact with a high ratio of losses.

Multiply these numbers to reflect both sides of the trade, the buy and the sell. For example, if you made three trades in a day and sold at the end of the day, you would have made six trades ($3 \times 2 = 6$). Most successful short-term traders trade within these conservative numerical ranges. If you are trading *less* than the conservative numbers, you probably have poor performance. You are being too cautious and may be afraid of losing. That's okay if you are a beginner, but after you have a year or two of real-time experience, you should achieve the conservative numbers.

The Optimum Potential Number

The optimum *potential* number assumes you would be making every single trade (buys and sells) based on the magic numbers. In this example, you are following three real-time securities; therefore, you have nine potential trading opportunities. Using the magic numbers, each security gives you three trading opportunities. This leaves us with the optimum number of trades, which, as you remember, is *nine* ($3 \times 3 = 9$). This number should not be exceeded on a trade-per-day basis.

In reality, you never take every single trade because every trade isn't a high-probability, high-profitability trade. You can use the optimum *potential* number to examine overtrading. If you exceed the optimum potential number, you are in all probability gambling. Remember that these numbers reflect the buy and the sell. To examine the number of individual buys or sells, simply divide the optimum potential numbers by 2. (See Table 3.2.)

By using a combination of the conservative numbers and the optimum potential numbers, you will be able to better examine your trading patterns. Remember to note the time of day you made the trade. This will become helpful in your analysis to ascertain whether you are trading when time-cycle volatility is in your favor.

Table 3.2 Optimum potential numbers

	Per Day	Per Week	Per Month	Per Year
Day trader	18	90	360	4,320
Microtrend trader		18	72	846
Position trader			18	276

It is also important because later, in Chapter 7, we will address key biological and psychological issues that affect trading.

The Mathematics of Trading and Commissions

Nothing supports the reasoning for not overtrading more than a look into the mathematics of what it takes to recover from the previous losing trade. Table 3.3 shows the percentage gain necessary to recover from a predetermined percentage loss. It is based on your initial investment capital. The obvious message from the table is that losses must be cut quickly. If not, they increase at a geometric rate.

The potential for loss is accelerated when *leverage* is used (margin, options, futures). It has been my experience that it is extremely difficult to recover from any loss of capital below 25 per-

Table 3.3 Recovering from a losing trade

Percent Loss of Capital	Percent Gain Required to Recover
5	5.3
10	11.1
15	17.6
20	25.0
25	33.3
30	42.9
35	53.8
40	66.7
45	81.8
50	100.0
55	120.0
60	150.0

cent. If you are using margin, and you have *two trades* that are down 20 percent, you must make more than 100 percent on the next two trades. Remember, you will have commission and slippage, which means that you need far more than 100 percent to break even. Risk and money management are of paramount importance to your success. I have known traders who have had 10 consecutive winning trades and lost it all by not managing the risk on two trades. When you enter a trade you become a *risk manager;* you are no longer a trader. *Never forget this.*

If you are *scalping* and making 30 or more trades a day, you had better be right almost all the time. Because of the number of trades you are making, your margin of error has to be very small. You can't afford to be wrong very often. Imagine, if you will, 5, 6, or 10 losing trades in a row. Who says a winning trade has to be followed by another winning trade? Every trader knows that a series of losses can happen at any time. Using Table 3.3, calculate what just three losing trades will do to you. Then figure the percentage of the impact if those trades are margin trades. Ouch! This information isn't in your account statement. Some traders reading this book right now are looking at their account statement and believe that they are making lots of money. In reality, they are already dead but they don't know it. Only drawdown analysis and creating an equity line will show you how good you really are as a trader. (See *Trading the Plan* by Deel.) You will never eliminate losses, but you should try to control drawdown. Your goal should be to never have a drawdown below 12 percent. This may be difficult to accomplish, but you should try to achieve this goal. This will force you to become a risk manager on every trade. What about commissions?

Commissions

Commissions are a fact of life and the cost of doing business. They affect your true profit and must be considered when performing a rate-of-return calculation. You must always remember to include the commission. Not including commissions in your calculations will give you a false picture of your rate of return and true profit potential. Unmanaged losses and commissions can make the difference between being a profitable trader and a losing trader. In many cases, individuals will try to cut the cost of their trading by looking for the cheapest commission around. Don't ever make the assumption that cheap is good. This is a lesson that the public never seems to learn and a professional understands all too well. It is especially true when it comes to commissions. I know companies that advertise commissions as low as $7 to $12. In fact, there are companies that will offer commission-free transactions. Always remember that you get what you pay for, and sometimes you get more than you bargained for. Let me explain how that $7 to $12 commission could cost you $512. In our example, you are buying a stock over the Internet using brokerage company A. The bid is $30 and the ask $30½. We are buying 1,000 shares and the spread is $500. At the same time, someone is selling the stock at the bid $30. What you don't know is that the second the order arrives at Internet broker A, A sells the order flow to firm B for $100 and charges you a $12 commission. Internet broker A just made $112 on your order. Let's look at what just happened. Because you were trading online over the Internet and not using ECNs, you did not have an option of narrowing the spread, so you did in fact lose money. You also had to pay a commission on the trade. Large spreads benefit market makers and firms involved in the practice of selling order flow. If you had been using an ECN, you could have posted an offer to buy at $30⅜ or 30¼, narrowing the spread and saving the difference. Using ECNs, you might have been able to buy on the bid, which is an opportunity that you will never experience online. Look at the breakdown of numbers to see how this transaction worked. Cheap commissions might be costing you a fortune. If someone offers to sell you a diamond ring for a dime and you buy it, you probably bought a diamond ring that isn't worth a dime.

Internet Broker Firm A	You Lose
$100.00 selling order flow	$500.00 spread
12.00 commission	12.00 commission
$+112.00 profit on transaction	$–512.00 lost on transaction

Companies can offer commission-free trading on certain stocks because the stocks usually have huge spreads of ⅜ to ½ point or more. Most of the time they make markets in these stocks or sell stock to you out of their inventory and make money on the spreads. Who needs to charge a commission? By not charging a commission, firms can always count on the something-for-nothing crowd to show up and buy. In this case the word *free* cost you $500. I would be happy to sell commission-free stock, because in a few years I would be very rich and you would be broke. When you hear the words *commission-free transactions,* someone is trying to sell you a 10 cent diamond ring.

Markets and Direction

Because markets are dynamic, you need to be able to adapt to current conditions. As a general prepares for battle, you need to select the correct strategy for your war between the bulls and the bears. Your enemy doesn't always fight using the same battle plan. You need to be flexible and ready to change when conditions do. Remember, the selection of trading strategy depends on the kind of trader you are, your time frame, and your own individual personality. It is important to understand that every trading strategy depends on the overall trend direction, strength, and duration of the markets. The two most important markets to you as a trader are the S&P 500 and the Nasdaq. If your trading vehicle is in the Nasdaq, you need to know the direction of that market. I have known traders to focus solely on the S&P 500. This is a mistake because the Nasdaq and the S&P 500 behave differently at times. Before you begin to make an individual trading decision, you need to establish what is taking place in *both* markets. If you are trading Internet stocks, you need to know what the Internet index is doing, as many times Internet stocks are driven by pure speculation. In a case like this, you need to know what the Internet index is doing. The S&P 500 and the Nasdaq could be going down while the Internet index is going up. No matter which markets you trade, you need to establish the overall market trend.

Identifying Market Trend

The first step after identifying the kind of trader you are is to establish the trend of the two most important markets for traders: the S&P 500 and Nasdaq. In both cases, you need an efficient way to visually and numerically quantify your analysis. With this information you will be able to review your data to identify current trends. This information can also be used in historical studies.

Market Trend Quantifier

The market trend quantifier is a simple but effective way of identifying the market trend, direction, duration, and strength. The quantifier requires you to input information into a spreadsheet or record data manually on the market trend quantifier worksheet. Doing this will alert you to small changes in trend.

The market trend quantifier uses a simple point system of +2, −2, or 0. For example, if the trend of the market is up and your intended trade is long in the direction of the market, then the score is +2. If the trend of the market is down and your intention is to short into that downward trend, your score will also be +2. The plus sign is a function of the direction of the trade that makes money. In this case both trades have a positive +2 score. However, if your intention is to buy into the market to go long (up) but the current trend is down, the score would be a −2. A score of 0 is obtained when the market is in a consolidation.

Refer to Figure 3.1, which shows an example of the market trend quantifier. Here's how to use it: Under Date, write in the current date. As a practical matter, you should do a market trend quantifier every two days. In the Market column, place the name of the market you are following (S&P 500, Nasdaq). In the Total Point Value column, you will place a numerical score, derived by subtracting the negative numbers from the positive numbers that make up the trend score in the Total Point Value column. This total will enable you to gauge the strength and duration of the markets you are following. In the Direction column, place an arrow indicating the direction of the market on that day. In the Action column, indicate a buy, sell, or hold decision. A glance at the market trend quantifier will enable you to ascertain all of this information on a given day. For

Figure 3.1 Market trend quantifier

Date	Market	Total Point Value	Direction ↑	Action

Positive Trend +2   Negative Trend –2   Neutral 0

example, on Tuesday the S&P 500 was in a strong upward trend, indicating a buy or a hold of current positions with strong correlation to the market.

The following items make up the market trend quantifier total point value:

Trendlines   +2, –2, 0

Exponential moving averages   20, 50, 150   +1, –1, 0

Money flow (14)   +1, –1, 0

RSI (14)   +1, –1, 0

TRIX (12)   +1, –1, 0

Support and resistance areas   +1, –1, 0

Interest rates   +1, –1, 0

The point value of trendlines has previously been explained. The maximum point value for moving averages is +3. To arrive at a +3 number for the point score would mean that price would have to be above all three moving averages. You could have a situation in which you were above the 150- (+1) and 50- (+1) day but below the 20- (–1) day moving average. In this case your point score would be +1, derived by subtracting the negative number from the positive numbers.

The money flow indicator will show movement into and out of the trading vehicle. A positive money flow reading would give you +1, a negative reading –1, and a neutral reading would be 0. When using the money flow indicator, use 14 days when asked for the time period.

Relative Strength Index (RSI) examines the internal strength of a stock, commodity, or market. Tops usually occur around or above 70 and bottoms near or below 30. Improving strength would be +1, while weakness would have a score of –1. Use 14 days when plotting the RSI indicator.

TRIX is a trend-following indicator. It displays the rate of change of a triple exponentially smoothed average of the close. Trix moves above and below a zero line. It also indicates the slope and angle of trend. If the trend is positive the score is +1, if negative –1. The time period for TRIX is 12 days.

Support and resistance lines are used if your trading vehicle is at or near one or the other. For example, if your trading vehicle is at support and beginning to move up, this would be +1. Conversely, if it is beginning to turn down, breaking support, your score would be –1. If there is no support or resistance reference, then the score would be 0.

Interest rates play an important role in the growth and strength of any investment vehicle. You would give +1 to an interest rate environment that is positive for the growth of the economy and –1 for negative interest rate factors. Focus on present rates and their relationship to historical lows and highs. Low rates are usually positive for the stock market, while high rates are traditionally not favorable for the market. Deflation is a low–interest rate environment that is negative for the economy and stocks.

All of the different factors in the market trend quantifier are totaled. If any negative numbers exist they are subtracted from the positive numbers and the resulting score is the total point value. By doing a market trend quantifier, you are always aware of the strength, duration, and direction of the market. Most trading vehicles have a strong correlation to the market direction and momentum.

Momentum Probability, Profitability Filter

This strategy is based on a series of logical assumptions. These assumptions should be equally true for the day trader, microtrend trader, and position trader. All traders should be trying to identify the highest-probability entry and exit points of a specific trading vehicle. The trading vehicle should have a positive correlation to the market in which it trades, and the trading vehicle should be in trend or beginning to trend. Given several different trading vehicle alternatives, you should be able to select the top three potential candidates for trading. This would include a reward-to-risk analysis, which would enable you to determine the profitability of each trade. To accomplish this you will need a filtering system to narrow down the field of trading candidates. Any database comprised of over 500 securities is overkill. Most beginning traders and aggressive investors load thousands of securities into their computers for analysis. They end up paying needless fees for the extra data and waste precious time doing analysis that usually goes nowhere. Your objective is to come up with three securities per day from which to select. If you remember, the magic numbers are three and five, with the optimum number being nine. The Momentum Probability, Profitability Filter (MPPF) uses this numerical balance in the following way. First, you must have a database of securities traded on the NYSE and the Nasdaq markets. This database should have no more than 500 securities in it. From your introduction to the conservative numbers, you know that you should have three trades per time cycle (day, week, month, year). If you take the number of securities in the database 500 and multiply it times the number of conservative trading opportunities (three) you will have 1,500 *potential* high-probability, profitability trades. Divide the number of trading days in a year (240) into the total number of potential trades (1,500), and you come up with 6.25 trades a day to select from. The next step is to select the three best potential candidates from those six and monitor them in real time. You now have three individual trading vehicles to monitor during the trading day, week, month, or year. If you are day trading, the maximum number of *entry trades* during any given day should not exceed nine. You can make a very good living making three to nine high-probability, profitability trades a day. The next question you should be asking yourself is, "What kind of screening process do I use to find these trading vehicles using this strategy?"

An examination of almost any chart will show you that most securities have three to five strong momentum trends over a period of a year. If you multiply this by the 500 securities in your database, you will begin to understand that you are looking for specific points in time when the security begins to move. As a trader, you don't care if the move is up or down—you just want a strong, sustained move. An analysis of Figure 3.2 will show you visually what you should be looking for. I have selected three trend runs over a period of a year and marked them with the arrows. These points are known as *momentum acceleration points.* Finding these momentum acceleration points is of the utmost importance. All securities exhibit them; the key is being able to find them. This can be accomplished by running a series of predetermined screening programs that filter through your database looking for bullish and bearish characteristics. Once you have several securities using your screening programs, you select the best of the list, narrowing it down to *three.* To accomplish this, you will use the trading trend quantifier.

**Figure 3.2   Momentum acceleration points
Chart courtesy of MetaStock®**

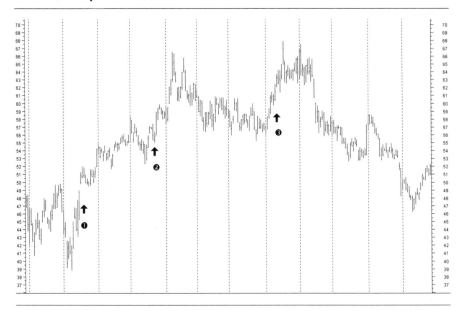

The Trading Trend Quantifier

The trading trend quantifier will enable you to select three highest-probability, profitability trading vehicles from a series of possible candidates. The _screens_ help you find the securities' momentum acceleration points. Momentum acceleration points represent the highest probability for success for the day trader, microtrend trader, or position trader. This point is the optimum entry or exit point for different time frames. Momentum acceleration points are of utmost importance, as they are the beginning of major trend runs, both positive and negative. I think it is extremely interesting that the entry point giving the highest probability for success is the same for an investor as it is for a day trader. This fact seems to have totally escaped the vast majority of day traders. You have to screen for momentum, and not just any momentum. You want to identify the _momentum acceleration points_ specific to each stock in your database.

The trading trend quantifier allows you to further analyze the candidates by allowing you to score them based on reward-to-risk ratio, trend strength, high-probability entry or exit, and sector strength. The best way to understand this process is to follow an example from beginning to end.

The Night Before the Trade

You are going to find that 90 percent of your money will come from the analysis you do the night before, not the day you make the trades. The moment the trade is placed, preparation meets opportunity. Don't just walk into your trading room the next day, turn on the computer, and act like a cowboy by shooting off trades at anything that moves. I tell my students, "Success is directly proportional to the amount of work you are willing to do that no one else will." If you become a day trading cowboy, your tombstone could read:

> Here lies the account of a cowboy trading master.
> He was fast on the mouse but somebody was faster.

At 7:00 P.M. you turn on your computer and begin to download your end-of-day data. This task is completed in a few minutes. End-of-day data? Yes, it is this data that you are going to run your filters on. Analyzing this information is the difference between success and failure in your real-time trading. Remember, you are looking for stocks that show *momentum acceleration points*. These points will reveal themselves in your analysis. The download now completed, open up your program and select the specific *exploration filters* you wish to apply to the database of 500 securities. These securities are on various exchanges. You select four screening programs, three looking for bullish characteristics and one for bearish. The first screen looks for stocks that have a 5 percent increase in price and a 30 percent increase in volume. The second seeks out stocks that have just broken above their 12-day exponential moving average. The third identifies stocks that show a buy signal from the Moving Average Convergence/Divergence (MACD) indicator. The fourth shows stocks that close below a 20-day moving average. After running the four screening programs, you open up each one and look at the list of securities generated in the report. Figure 3.3 shows your first filter.

You select a chart from the security list and open the chart for a quick look. Many times this is all you have to do to eliminate it from your master list. The master list is generated when you have made your total selection from all four screens. Understand that you can have many different screens. I am using four to illustrate how the process works and how to apply the trading trend quantifier once the selections have been made. Figure 3.4 shows stocks breaking above their 12-day exponential moving average (EMA).

A move in momentum accompanied by a close above the 12-day exponential moving average (EMA) is of importance. My studies of trend and momentum have shown that if price moves above the

Figure 3.3   5 percent increase in price, 30 percent increase in volume
Chart courtesy of MetaStock®

FInvestment Tech Group	65.5000	60.1880	8.8257	2699.0000
HMicron Tech	68.9380	64.0000	7.7156	79252.0000
HMicrosoft Corp.	92.1880	86.4380	6.6522	602060.0000
M1Chrion Corp	33.0000	31.3750	5.1793	49150.0000

Figure 3.4 Breakout above a 12-day EMA
Chart courtesy of MetaStock®

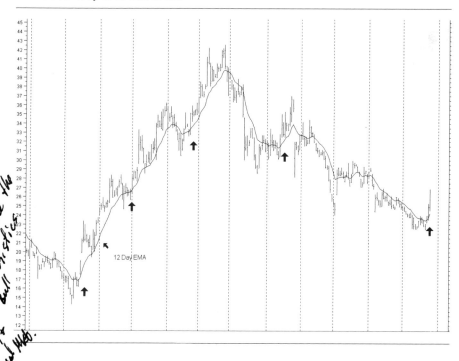

12 Day EMA

What are the Characteristics in a Bull ~ Bear, r neutral mkt.

12-day EMA, very often trend will run for three to five days in the *///* direction of the breakout. Major trend moves tend to begin when price moves above or below the 12-day EMA.

The MACD is a trend-following indicator and is one of the indicators you use to help you make a high-probability entry or exit decision (see Figure 3.5). Remember, one indicator does not supersede another. A buy or sell decision is derived by the total score, which takes into consideration all indicators.

Figure 3.6 is a bearish screen, but it has bullish potential if stocks rebound off the moving average or support. This screen needs to be evaluated from both perspectives: bullish and bearish.

Once you have reviewed all four screens, you select several possible securities that you place in your master list. From this list you begin the process of elimination. When you view chart data, make sure you are viewing one year of price information. The steps

Figure 3.5 MACD indicator buy signal list
Chart courtesy of MetaStock®

Security Name	Close	MACD	Previous	Mov Ave
AO Reilly Auto	39.5940	-2.2135	-2.3379	-2.2928
CAnheuser Bush	77.3750	0.4434	0.3719	0.3863
CGillette Co.	46.0630	0.2307	0.1388	0.1790
CWrigley	76.3750	-2.1122	-2.3550	-2.2898
F1General Mills	84.1250	0.2379	0.1734	0.1963
FFed Nat Mtg Ass	65.3130	-0.8520	-0.9853	-0.9036
HAmerican BK NT Holographic	2.3130	-0.1704	-0.2084	-0.1738
IJohnson Controls	70.2500	0.2999	0.2829	0.2979
MAccess Health Inc	37.5630	0.5631	0.4859	0.5198
MArterial Vascular Inc	58.3750	1.6119	1.3108	1.5579
OBritish Petrol	90.7500	-0.1253	-0.3179	-0.1888
OChevron Corp.	95.9380	0.4361	0.4132	0.4207
RLTC Properties	11.3750	-0.3021	-0.3183	-0.3113
TMCI	59.3120	-1.3629	-1.5574	-1.5103

Figure 3.6 Bearish-bullish filter
Chart courtesy of MetaStock®

Security Name	Ticker ...
AGenuine Parts	GPC
ASonic Automotive CLA	SAH
CAbercrombis Fitch Co	ANF
CEducational Management	EDMC
CGoodrich Co	GR
CINt. Flav Fryan	IFF
CMicro Warehouse Inc	MWHS
COffice Depot	ODP
COutback Steakhouse	OSSI
CPetsmart Inc	PETM
CPixar Inc	PIXR
CWalgreen	WAG
EThermo Inst Sys	THI
F!Safweay Inc	SWY

in this process are listed in order. The securities that remain after this screen will be further eliminated using the trading trend quantifier.

1. *Trendlines:* Draw in the major trendlines on the chart. Do not identify every change in trend, just major trend moves as shown in Figure 3.7.

2. *Support and resistance:* Begin at the bottom of the chart and draw in your support and resistance lines, working your way to the top of the chart. Remember, the chart must show one year of price data for you to do your analysis. (See Figure 3.8.)

After identifying your support and resistance lines, use them to calculate the next step of the process of elimination: the reward-to-risk Ratio (see Figure 3.9).

Figure 3.7   Trendlines
Chart courtesy of MetaStock®

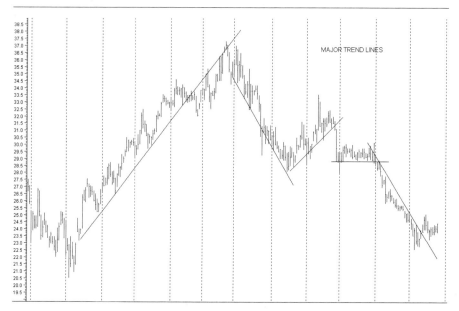

Figure 3.8 Support and resistance
Chart courtesy of MetaStock®

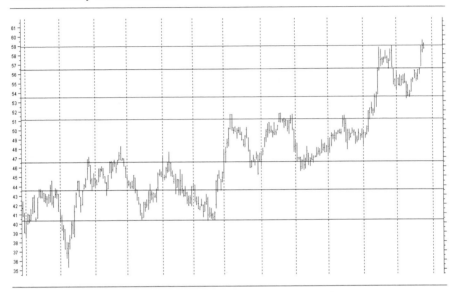

You will note that you are doing a calculation based on daily price bars and one year's worth of data. You are looking for a reward-to-risk ratio of 2.5 or better. Identifying this ratio is very important for all short-term traders. If the reward-to-risk ratio is 2.5 or greater, then you will proceed with the analysis. If it is less, then you will eliminate the stock at once. Don't ever make the mistake of trading a stock just because the trade has a high probability of success. I have witnessed many cases where traders lost because there wasn't any money in the trade to begin with. As a short-term trader, you need maximum profitability potential on every trade you make. As you know, every trade is not a winner, so common sense dictates taking only those trades that have the most profit potential. By doing a reward-to-risk ratio in this manner you will find trades with the potential to move several points. If you risk money only when the potential profit is 2.5 times greater than the risk and use strict risk and money management principles, you will survive while others perish.

If a stock has a 2.5 or better reward-to-risk ratio, you can proceed with the application of other technical indicators. Each indica-

Figure 3.9   Support and resistance
Chart courtesy of MetaStock®

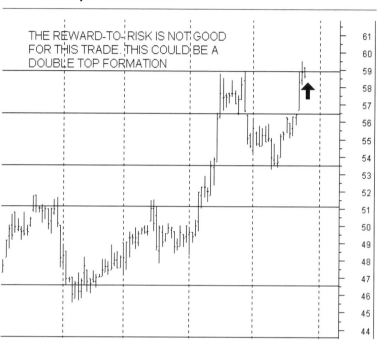

THE REWARD-TO-RISK IS NOT GOOD
FOR THIS TRADE. THIS COULD BE A
DOUBLE TOP FORMATION

tor has a point system assigned to it. All indicators have a point value of +1, −1, or 0. By giving all the indicators the same numerical weight, the stock with the largest point value and reward-to-risk ratio is first on your list. This eliminates emotional decisions and personal biases toward any one stock. At this point you input the information into the trading trend quantifier.

Using the Trading Trend Quantifier

The trading trend quantifier enables you to find the three stocks with the highest profitability and probability out of a large number of selections. If, for example, you had ten stocks using this simple method, it is possible to narrow the list down to the top three. The trading trend quantifier divides analysis of a potential trading vehicle the following ways.

First, the reward-to-risk ratio is entered in the R/R column. Second, a trend score is given to each of the potential candidates, along with the direction of the trend, which is indicated by an arrow up, down, or sideways. This number and the arrow are placed in the trend column. Third, all technical indicators are totaled, subtracting the negative from the positive numbers. The total is jotted down on a piece of paper. This number represents high-probability buy or sell signals. Fourth, the trend score and the high-probability score are added together and the number is entered in the total point value column. In the fifth and last step, the action column is filled in with a decision: B = Buy, S = Sell, H = Hold.

High-probability buy and sell signals and their numerical values are as follows:

Moving averages   12, 20, 50   +1, –1, 0
MACD   +1, –1, 0
RSI (14)   +1, –1, 0
Rate of change   12, 26, 39   +1, –1, 0
Bollinger bands   +1, –1, 0
Williams % R   +1, –1, 0

I suggest you use the trading trend quantifier to input the information. Place the data in a three-ring binder for easy access and review. This will become useful in later analysis. (See Figure 3.10.)

After the information is entered into the trading trend quantifier, it is a simple matter to select the stocks that have the highest reward-to-risk ratio, trend score, and total score. Note that the total score is a combination of trend and high-probability buy and sell indicators. You may enter the information into a spreadsheet to expedite the process. Using this simple method eliminates emotional decisions and results in the three stocks with the best potential out of a list of selections.

The Momentum Probability, Profitability Filter is an excellent trading strategy. By using this method you are selecting stocks based on momentum and profitability. This strategy will work well

Figure 3.10 **Trading trend quantifier**

Date	Vehicle	Total Point Value	Trend	R/R	Action
Today	IBM	17	7 ↑	3.0	Buy

Trend Score		**Entry and Exit Indicators**	
Trendlines	+2	**Moving averages (12, 20, 50)**	**+3**
Moving averages	+3	**MACD**	**+1**
Support and resistance	0	**RSI (14-day)**	**+1**
Chart patterns	+1	**Price rate of change (12, 26, 39)**	**+3**
Volume	+1	**Bollinger bands**	**+1**
		Williams % R	**+1**
Total	+7		**+10**
Total score = 17			

in all market conditions because the filter and screening process will find bullish and bearish *momentum acceleration points*. While this strategy works well in bullish and bearish markets, you need more than one strategy.

Trading the Basket and the Sectors

From a trading desk, a loud voice screams, "Sell the stocks and buy the futures!" Later in the day that same voice announces, "Buy the futures and sell the stocks!" With the push of a button, a basket of hundreds of stocks are sold in the blink of an eye. This is a game that is played by portfolio managers and arbitrageurs every day in an attempt to balance the risk of their positions and to profit by the move. Based on what they believe fair value to be and the "premium" or "spread," they *buy undervalue* and *sell overvalue*. Fair value is simply the value of the S&P 500 plus interest paid minus all dividends. If the futures price is too high relative to the present index value, arbitrageurs and others can buy diversified portfolios of stocks of large companies and sell equivalent amounts of overpriced stock index futures. The reverse can be accomplished by pushing the sell button. In most cases, human beings are not pushing the buttons to buy or sell. Computers are buying and selling based on a valuation program. This is what is referred to as *program trading* or *index arbitrage*. This selling and buying moves the market, specific stocks, and sectors. A short-term trader can take advantage of this massive buying and selling.

Before the market opens, a trader using the basket strategy would find out if the futures were trading at a premium or a discount. This will give the trader an idea of market trend direction for a short period of time.

The Trading Basket

The strategy works by trading stocks within the basket that duplicate the S&P 500 stock index. When buy and sell programs hit the market, the stocks within the basket move. This momentum will drive *a few* of the stocks within the basket in a trend direction for an hour or more. This strong trend move is what basket traders are looking for, and most stocks will be impacted for a short period of time, moving fractions of a point. The basket trader wants to identify the few stocks in the group that will have a sustained trend, giving the trader potential points over a short period of time. Many times, the stocks that move like this represent early moves into or out of key sectors.

The second part to this strategy is to create baskets of stocks, each holding three of the top stocks in a specific sector. A total of ten sectors are represented and are divided into two groups of five sectors with three stocks in each basket. The total number of stocks in all baskets is 30. The baskets can be further divided into 15 stocks on the NYSE and 15 on Nasdaq markets. Some basket traders increase the number of stocks to 60 by building two different basket groups, 30 holding stocks on NYSE and 30 holding stocks on the Nasdaq.

If you know which sectors are showing strength or weakness, you can use this information to your advantage. Having already constructed the sector baskets, you can find stocks to trade long or short. Taking advantage of both program arbitrage and sector rotation makes trading baskets a viable strategy to consider.

Building a Basket

The first step in building a basket is to select the stocks that will come close to duplicating the index. This is made simpler because you are placing the top three stocks in each of your 10 sectors. In most cases, this will approximate the stocks that are part of program arbitrage. It should become obvious that it is possible for you to do some arbitrage of your own by going long in one sector and shorting in another. In most cases, you are looking for the *top three stocks* out of all of the stocks in the basket. Once momentum is found, you trade that momentum until it ends.

Part of building a basket is to input into your computer the various indices that coincide to the sector you are building—for example, the Semiconductor Index known by the symbol SOX. If you are trading Intel or Micron Technology, you need to know not only what the market is doing but the Semiconductor Index as well. This is true for all stocks. An excellent example of the importance of knowing how the index is trading is Internet stocks. The S&P 500 and the Nasdaq might be in a strong downtrend for the day while Internet stocks are trending up. An examination of the Internet index symbol INX would confirm this trend, which is counter to the market. Indices can be charted to give you a visual image of the index trend. Using moving averages, RSI, and other indicators, you can establish the strength of that trend on a given day or over a specific period of time.

Here is an example of five baskets, each divided into a specific sector. Another set of five sectors will complete the total basket of 30 stocks. Identified by their symbols from left to right, the sectors are Computer Hardware, Semiconductors, Food, Telecommunications, and Pharmaceutical.

IBM	INTC	SLE	T	MRK
DELL	MU	CPB	LU	PFE
CPQ	NSM	HNZ	QCOM	ABT

I suggest that you build your baskets out of the top stocks in the various indices. One stock that you will want to include is General Electric (symbol GE). If you print out a chart of GE and superimpose the S&P 500 over it you will see that GE and the S&P 500 are almost congruent. When the programs are selling GE, it goes down. When they buy GE, it usually goes up. Here is a small list of stocks, identified by their stock symbol, that will more than likely be found in buy and sell programs.

IBM	KO	WMT
CPQ	PEP	DH
HWP	VO	JCP
DELL	BUD	S

MSFT	CPB	G
ORCL	HNZ	PG
NOVL	K	CL
CA	SLE	MTC

BAC	MOB	INTC
CCI	ARC	MU
WB	XON	MOT
BKB	CHV	ORCL

T	F	AMGN
QCOM	GM	BGEN
ATI	GPC	BMET
SBC	GT	GENZ

The Most Actives

The most actives list of stocks show the most shares traded on a given day. Stocks that make the most active list are stocks with unusually high trading volume. This activity can be caused by takeover activity, earning releases, institutional trading in specific issues, and other factors. Institutional trading in some cases can alert you to early moves into or out of specific sectors. Be aware that a news event could kill a profit.

Most activities can sometimes exhibit extreme volatility, while at other times the price movement is slow and volatility is almost nonexistent. Traders who trade the most activities as one of their trading strategies are in most cases experienced traders. This strategy requires a fluid, unemotional focus. You must be quick to react to trend change, and you need a thorough understanding of the market trend and sector rotation. The majority of traders who use this strategy are day traders. They are looking for a short-term trend in one direction or another. This will enable them to enter a trade long or short.

Aggressive investors can use this strategy because the most active stocks are the beginning of a move into or out of a specific sector. Noting the direction of this trend and analyzing the stocks that are trending will enable you to identify long-term sector rotation. Watch for follow-through of trend from the day before. Ask yourself if this is the beginning, middle, or end of a trend move. Many times, a trader can take a position in these stocks for several days. As the trend continues into weeks, you can enter long or short the stock. *Whenever you take a position that you intend to hold overnight you must place an exit stop.* There is no exception to this rule. Despite all of your bullish analysis and understanding of the market, your stock can go lower. By placing a stop you are limiting a loss or locking in a profit. If you are trading electronically, you must exit at a predefined point.

Most trading software will give you the ability to look up the most actives on the NYSE, Nasdaq, and AMEX. Some will allow you to access the most active options as well. If you do not have this information, call any broker to find out which stocks are the most active for the day.

The 20 Most Volatile Stocks

This strategy is for the more experienced trader. Electronic traders will enjoy this strategy because they have the technology to take advantage of quick changes in price trend. This strategy requires you to be able to react to price momentum very quickly and is primarily for day traders, options traders, and some microtrend traders. This strategy is not appropriate for aggressive investors who typically hold a position for two weeks or more. If you are using this strategy as a microtrend trader, you must use stops, for a microtrend trader will not hold one of these stocks over five days.

By using screening, you can filter for the most volatile stocks in your database over the past 10 days. This will give you a field of long and short selections. After you review the charts, you will select *three* of the most volatile that seem to be moving in a definable trend, either up or down. *Do not* try to trade this strategy using online brokers. Because of the interday volatility on these stocks, if you are wrong you must be able to exit the trade with as small a loss as possible, and only electronic traders will have the ability to enter and exit within seconds. Figures 3.11 to 3.13 are charts of stocks that appeared in the most volatile screen. All screens, strategies, and formulas are given to students of tradingschool.com.

Note that all three stocks show volatility and trend. Instead of trying to scalp fractions of a point (e.g., $\frac{1}{16}$ or $\frac{1}{8}$), you can use this and the other strategies to trade for $\frac{1}{2}$ or several points. The key to trading this strategy is to identify the trend strength and trade in that direction.

Trading Closed-End Funds

This has to be one of the best kept secrets on Wall Street. I have been trading closed-end funds since 1989. They are, for the most part, boringly predictable, which is just what you want if you want to make money. You would think that all traders, especially professional traders, would know about trading closed-end funds, but this is not the case.

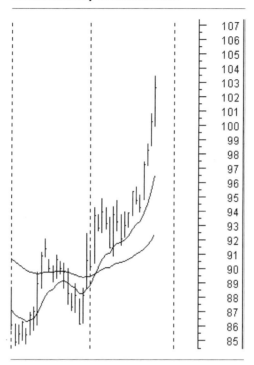

Figure 3.11   Volatile stock from filter
Chart courtesy of MetaStock®

One day after trading, several colleagues got together to talk about the market and what we had planned for the next day. (I'm convinced that the real reason we got together at this particular place was because of the delicious hors d'oeuvres.) One of the traders for another firm asked me what I was trading, and I told him closed-end funds. "What for?" he said. "They don't have any volatility. How can you make any money doing that?" He then proceeded to give me a 15-minute lecture on the error of my ways. After sharing his wisdom with me, he made a strategic move toward the hors d'oeuvres table, where I overheard him giving some other misguided trader the benefit of his advice. I just did not have the heart to tell him that I had made enough money trading those boring closed-ends funds to buy hors d'oeuvres for the next 10,000 years!

Figure 3.12   Volatile stock from filter
Chart courtesy of MetaStock®

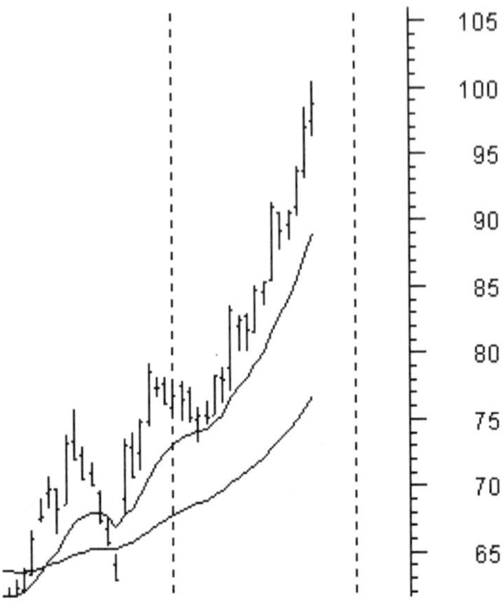

Even on Wall Street, traders become victims of their own egos and lack of knowledge. The same is true with electronic trading.

What Is a Closed-End Fund?

Before I explain the strategy of how to trade closed-end funds in the short term, you need to learn some basic information about closed-end funds. A closed-end fund, unlike a mutual fund, has a fixed number of shares. These funds trade over the exchange like stocks. One of the interesting things about closed-end funds is their ability to trade at a discount or a premium in relation to their true value. This occurs on a frequent basis due to inefficient market valuation. As with any stock, at times it is considered undervalued (i.e., worth more than the price at which it is currently trading). Let me explain this in the following way. If you could buy a pool of assets (fund) worth $1 at a 20 percent discount, would you do it? Put another way, for every 80 cents you spent, you would be buying $1.20 in real value. The extra 20 cents is the unrealized discount on the asset

---

**Figure 3.13 Volatile stock from filter
Chart courtesy of MetaStock®**

pool. If you really think about it, buying a closed-end fund and pay-ing a commission would be far better than buying a no-load mutual fund. When you buy a no-load fund you are buying a dollar's worth of assets for a dollar. Closed-end funds offer many advantages over mutual funds and common stocks. Let's list some other advantages of closed-end funds.

1. Closed-end funds statistically outperform mutual funds. This should get the attention of people who try to time mutual funds.

2. You always know the selling and buying price of a closed-end fund because it trades on the exchange like a stock. If you think about it, buying a mutual fund is an act of faith, because you never know what price you are going to pay. The net asset value (NAV) of a mutual fund is derived after

the close of the market day. You do not know what price you paid until the next day.

3. Closed-end funds can be purchased for substantial discounts from their present value. You can not accomplish this with mutual funds. In fact, most mutual funds, even no-load mutual funds, have hidden fees associated with them. Many times, that no-load fund is really costing you money—you just do not know it.

4. Closed-end funds offer liquidity that simply does not exist with mutual funds. For example, let us suppose the market is moving down 570 points based on the Dow and you want to sell. If you own a mutual fund, you cannot get out until the end of the day. What if, at the end of the day, the market is down 870 points? Ouch! When the market fell in October 1987, some people panicked and sold their funds. Even though the market did come back, several funds took years to recover a one-day loss. Even the best of funds felt the effects of Black Monday. Ask Peter Lynch, whose Fidelity Magellan fund lost one-third of its value that day. Being able to sell a closed-end fund intraday offers tremendous advantages over a mutual fund from a risk and money management viewpoint.

5. Index options can be used to hedge positions of the closed-end funds in a much more cost-effective way.

6. Closed-end funds give you the ability to leverage a position with the use of margin. This is very advantageous for traders because closed-end funds, for the most part, while not extremely volatile, do tend to trend strongly in one direction or another.

7. Closed-end funds can be sold short. If you think about this, you can envision ways to hedge your positions that you might not have thought of before.

8. You can create spread arbitrage by buying one closed-end fund at a discount and selling another short at a premium.

By now you should realize that these boring funds have some amazing potential. The information you have received thus far can be used to improve your trading in various ways. Let us now look at how you trade closed-end funds.

How You Trade Closed-End Funds

The observation that closed-end funds are not ordinarily volatile is true. However, closed-end funds tend to trend intraday and over long periods of time. Once you understand this, you should see an opportunity. One of the reasons scalping has such a high failure rate is because of massive volatility. While this attracts the speculator and the get-rich-quick crowd, *you* do not want this kind of attention. If you are going to make money trading small fractions of points, then repeat after me: "Boring is good." Because *boring* typically translates into predictable slow-moving trend. Real money is made quietly in the background, almost unnoticed, trade by trade. In this kind of trading environment it is quite possible to trade for fractions of a point because the reward-to-risk ratio is in your favor. In fact, the very lack of volatility is just what an individual trading for ⅛ or ¼ point wants. Volatility and attention are the last things you need when your profit margin is small. Let the day trading cowboys have all the hype and attention they can get, because they are not going to make much money. If you are the only one eating your lunch, you just might be able to enjoy it. But if 20 people are fighting over your sandwich, you will be very lucky to get even a crumb. I like to eat my lunch alone and profit from the experience.

Many closed-end funds are traded on NYSE, which means you will be using the Super DOT system to place your order. This superior tool is available only to electronic traders. In *most* cases, you can place a trade and get confirmation within three to six seconds. I will address Super DOT and electronic communication networks and how to use them in Chapter 6.

When you trade closed-end funds, you are looking for a wide spread between the bid and the ask. This will not go unnoticed by professional traders, so you must move quickly to take advantage of the situation. We are assuming there is an upward basis in trend to carry you into a position where you will be able to sell the stock for a fraction of a point higher than you bought it. If the spread is large enough, you split the bid and the ask. For example, if the *bid* is 12 and the *ask* is 12¼, you can place a bid of 12⅛. If you succeed and are filled, you now become part of the national best bid or offer (NBBO). The idea is to turn right around and do one of the following: You can offer the closed-end fund at 12¼ with the crowd. If momentum is strong you can hold and sell it at 12⁵⁄₁₆ or 12⅜. Most of the time, you offer stock at a price you know will sell right away. In this case, you want to sell it at the *ask* 12¼. Closed-end funds and individual stocks offer a much lower risk factor when trading for fractions if volatility is minimal. Boring is good.

The problem with all strategies in which you are trying to trade for fractions of a point is size. By *size* I am talking about trading 1,000 to 2,000 shares of a specific trading vehicle. Closed-end funds are no different in this regard than an individual stock. Because the profit is so small, to make money you have to buy large numbers of shares. In the example, you will have over $12,000 in one trade. If this seems large to you, then you should reassess your trading capital. One of the biggest problems traders face is being undercapitalized. Capital is particularly important when you are trading for small fractions (¹⁄₁₆ to ⅛) of a point. Because the profit potential is so small, you are forced to allocate large amounts of capital to each individual trade. If this strategy is to succeed, you must use strict risk and money management principles to control loss.

Capital Requirements

His heart was pounding so loudly that he was certain the trader next to him could hear it. As his hand rested on the mouse, it trembled with apprehension. Suddenly, a cry went around the trading room, "There goes the S&P!" As the market dropped, so did his confidence. The next sound was the click of the mouse. Seconds seemed like an eternity. The confirmation came back: *Sold.* Without thinking, he uttered under his breath, "What am I doing?" Being undercapitalized for trading will only add to your anxiety. Most individual traders do not have enough capital in reserve for drawdown. The novice traders place almost all of their capital into one or two trades because greed drives them to make the big killing. Usually, they are the only ones getting killed. You always know who they are because you hear them from across the room, howling in pain. If you are going to trade electronically you need to have enough capital in reserve to neutralize runaway fear and anxiety. The very *minimum* an electronic trader should have is $50,000. If you feel heart-pounding fear and anxiety every time you place a trade, you probability do not have enough trading capital. Please do not trade until you do. Remember, it takes money to make money.

One of the problems of trading closed-end funds is that intraday charts on the funds are, for the most part, extremely poor. When doing analysis on closed-end funds, look at daily price information over six months to a year. Using technical indicators, trendlines, moving averages, and volume will assist you in finding the highest-probability entry point. Because intraday chart information is so poor with closed-end funds, you have to watch the bid and ask prices and the ticker for trend direction. A technical indicator that is useful in establishing trend is a one-minute momentum of price. This indicator can be used on stocks and commodities. Because intraday price information does not translate well into a bar chart of closed-end funds, it may be better to rely on short-term intraday moving averages rather than on price bars to help visually identify price trend.

The California Raiders: Piranha Traders

The California Raiders is not a football team. It is a group of 25 traders who every trading day at 6:30 A.M. Pacific time begin a raid on the stocks traded on the NYSE. They do not stop their attack until the final bell. When they finish, the only things left are the bones of the traders they went after on the floor of the exchange. The California Raiders are what I term *piranha traders*. They trade for fractions—⅛ here, ¼ there—and take small bites of their prey. They can attack a stock en masse when they sense weakness, and when they do they can bring a stock down one bite at a time. Once first blood has been drawn by the piranha traders, other traders join the feeding frenzy, each wanting a pound of flesh. Once they start, they absolutely will not stop until the closing bell. Who are these raiders who strike a stock without warning? The California Raiders are made up of a group of former floor specialists known as *rogue traders* by their peers. A rogue trader is a specialist or former professional trader who has found it more profitable to trade on his or her own than from the floor of the exchange. The raiders also are made up of superior traders who have proved their ability by making millions of dollars. They trade with almost unlimited amounts of capital at their disposal. Just one of the raiders may trade over a million shares in a single day. A few of the raiders are *biomechanical traders* which you will learn about in Chapter 7.

If you are going to trade using a scalping strategy, you are going to trade against market makers, specialists, and traders like the California Raiders. Remember, 92 percent of scalpers lose money. If for some unknown reason you have to trade for fractions, look for slow-moving stocks with intraday trend. It may not be exciting—but boring is better than broke.

Twenty-Five Old Friends

This strategy requires that you rotate the stocks when the sector is no longer in favor. Over time, you will find 25 stocks that you know very well and can trade with confidence. You will come to regard these 25 stocks as old friends. If other strategies do not seem to work, you can always rely on your old friends. Take them out for a trade or two.

Old friends are stocks that you have come to know very well over the course of several years of trading. Because of your experience with the stocks, you know their chart movements, support and resistance, overbought/oversold areas, and have a feel for where the price will move. Be careful: Limiting yourself to a few stocks will result in missing profitable moves in others. Do *not* marry a stock. You know that a trader has married a stock when you hear him or her say, "I love the company." For this strategy to work, you must select five of the major stocks in five sectors that are currently in favor. Most of the time, only three sectors will be obviously in play. The stocks you want will have institutional following, which will result in enough volatility for you to trade them successfully. This strategy is obviously not a strategy in which you trade for small fractions of a point. You will be trading stocks in half- or full-point increments. You can day trade, microtrend trade, or aggressively invest using this strategy.

Let's review the steps in this trading strategy:

1. Identify the five leading and lagging sectors.

2. Find the top five stocks in the sectors.

3. Follow those stocks and get to know them well.

4. Trade the stocks that exhibit the most momentum. I suggest you use the following technical indicators to measure momentum and strength: price rate of change, Relative Strength Index (RSI) and ADX to measure trend strength.

5. When the sector and momentum fall out of favor, look for opportunities to sell short.

6. Look for new sectors that show bullish strength.

Selecting a Strategy

When you select a strategy, you first must know what kind of trader you are and what your time frame is. If you make a buy or sell decision as a day trader, you cannot then use the trading plan of a microtrend trader by saying "I will hold it for the long term" if the plan goes against you.

After you read over the various strategies, select two that fit your personality and trading ability. Remember, while some of the strategies work in most stock market cycles, you need to thoroughly understand more than one strategy and how to apply it. Electronic trading gives you the ability to enter or exit bullish and bearish trends with surgical precision. The technology enables you to control risk and manage money as never before. For this reason, the use of electronic trading is part of every strategy you select. Electronic trading is *not* just for scalping. Microtrend traders, position traders, and even aggressive investors can use this technology and the strategies in this chapter to help improve their success. Remember the magic numbers, and don't exceed the optimum number of trades for the day trader, microtrend trader, or aggressive investor.

Do not fall into the trap of not allowing enough time to test the strategy you select. The best traders in the world let the market come to them. Most of the time, you will sit and watch for the entry or exit opportunity to materialize. Remember, every day is not a high-probability trading day. Make time your friend instead of your enemy.

chapter 4

a picture is worth a thousand words

An analysis of price movement will show that stocks and markets move in distinctive, identifiable trends. These trends exist in multiple time frames of minutes, hours, weeks, months, even years. The existence of these trends is what high-probability, profitability traders and aggressive investors are seeking to identify. Once a trend is identified, the trader or aggressive investor can quickly evaluate the opportunity and take action. Your success in trading short- and long-term time frames will depend on your ability to absorb and process visual information. For example, when you look at a painting your mind absorbs vast amounts of visual information: the shape of the frame, colors, textures, dimension, angles, and more. You observe and record all of this data within the blink of an eye. Bar charts hold countless pieces of critical information for the trained eye to see. Successful traders then translate this information into physical action, resulting in a buy or sell decision. The problem is that most information on short-term trading, particularly electronic trading, does not emphasize the importance of technical analysis. The focus is on scalping. Most scalpers think technical analysis is not relevant when, in fact, this is not the case: It is of the utmost importance.

One of the keys to successful short-term trading is an understanding of bullish and bearish chart patterns and trends. Learning how to read *real-time charts* is almost never covered, and it is critical to your success. In this chapter we are going to examine specific price movement and information, which will be very new to most of you. This is because reading and interpreting charts in real time is *different* in many ways from classical chart analysis. In some cases, the traditional interpretation is the exact opposite of what you would expect. Before I discuss the various patterns and their characteristics, let me explain why you want and need this information.

Great traders identify trend and stay with it until it reverses. They *do not* abandon trend after it moves up $\frac{1}{16}$ or $\frac{1}{8}$ of a point. In day trading, for example, trends usually sustain themselves over various time intervals. The most common time periods for stock trends to run are 15 minutes, 20 minutes, 35 minutes, and one hour. When stocks begin a strong intraday run, they will usually trend in one direction for one of the four time periods. During this trend, there could be downward movement in one or two of the price bars, but the trend will usually keep moving upward or downward until the trend reverses. Because trend is usually of a longer duration, you have the potential to capture substantial capital in one trade. You could have a very nice profit and pay little in commission compared to the scalper who is making a tremendous number of trades. Let us assume that the one-way commission is $20 for the scalper and for you. *Your* total commission is $120, which represents three buys and three sells. The *scalper* has a commission of $800, which represents 20 buys and 20 sells. Because the scalper is making far more trades, the potential to lose money on each individual trade is magnified by the number of trades. The result could be a loss of thousands of dollars, which does not include the commission. I know traders who make only three to five high-probability trades who have a nice profit at the end of the trading day. Compare this to the scalper who lost large amounts of capital and paid far more in commissions. Never be fooled into thinking by taking more trades you will make more money. I prefer to take three to five high-probability trades over twenty scalping trades on every occasion. If you think about it, this is just common sense. When it comes to day trading, it has been my experience that logic and common sense are abandoned for emotional trading driven by fear and greed. For you to trade with the trend and use a high-probability entry and exit strategy, you must know how to read both long-term and intraday charts. Without an understanding of technical analysis and rigid adherence to the trading plan, your success in trading will be minimal.

The Aura of Volatility

Most of us are familiar with the concept of electromagnetic fields. You cannot see them, but they exist and exert influence on objects that surround them. The electromagnetic fields that surround magnets have defined boundaries and shape. To see them, place a strong bar magnet under a piece of paper. On top of the paper, sprinkle iron filings. Like magic, these iron filings will stand upright and take shape around the positive and negative poles of the magnet.

If you look at an individual price bar for a given day you see the high, low, close, and open for that day. Most people just see these bits of information and go no further. But as with the magnet, there is an invisible force that surrounds each daily price bar. The invisible force is *intraday volatility*. Volatility shapes the bar's high-low range, dictates the trend, and influences the other price bars. Each bar has to some degree an influence on the future price movement the next day. Because of this, you need to ascertain the intraday price movement of the previous day. In some cases you might want to observe the intraday movement of the previous five days. This will give you a feel for what traders are doing. For example, you may find intraday support and resistance levels that carry over into the next day. This trading behavior could give you clues that reveal whether a market maker or an institutional trader was taking positions or was a net seller of the stock at specific price levels.

When you see an individual price bar or a group, look beyond the high, low, open, and close. Remember that each bar will have a given intraday volatility. This will help you in entering and exiting the trade. It is also important when placing a protective stop. There are several specific things to keep in mind in regard to intraday volatility:

1. Bisect the high-low range of an individual price bar by making a dotted line across the middle of the high-low price range.

2. Is the close above or below the middle of the high-low price range?

3. Did it close toward the low or the high of the range?

4. Where is the open in relation to the close on each given day?

Figure 4.1 shows high-low range analysis. This information is important because it can give you an idea of potential trend movement. Examine five days of data and note the relationship of the close above and below the midline. Is it closer to the high or the low? It is also important to note whether you are nearing a support or resistance area—not intraday support or resistance, but resistance based on daily price bars.

The close on this specific day was above the midline of the high-low price range and toward the high of the day. The day closed on a bullish bias. Note that the opening price was near the low of the day. When you see this kind of representation, you can feel confident that the trend for the day was bullish. The price range from high to

Figure 4.1   Bisecting high-low range

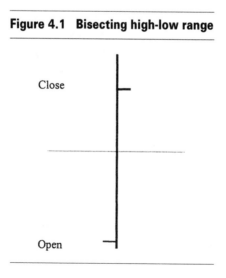

low will indicate the bullishness of one day compared to another day. I would suggest that you add the price range of the high and low for each of five days and then divide the total by the number of days. By doing this you will have an idea of the average price range for a week. (See Figures 4.2 and 4.3.) The intraday volatility shows the price movement based on a given day, which represents the aura of volatility that surrounds all daily price movement.

Figure 4.2 shows the range volatility for a period of five days. Note the open and close relationships. The majority of the price action for this five-day period was bearish. In this example, you also had a series of lower highs and lower lows. Of course, this does not have to be the case. If the stock was not trending as dramatically, as shown in Figure 4.2, you might not notice a bearish setup. This is why your focus should be on the open and close relationships of each daily price bar.

Figure 4.2   Daily range volatility

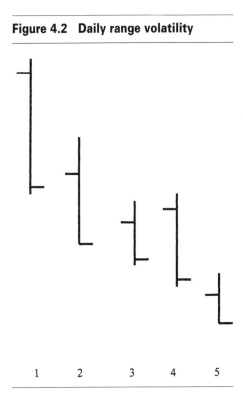

1   2   3   4   5

You will want to ascertain the average price volatility for the week and then record this information for possible future reference if you plan to trade this stock on an ongoing basis. In Figure 4.2 the daily high-low price range for each of the five days was as follows:

Day 1	$2.50
Day 2	2.25
Day 3	1.25
Day 4	2.00
Day 5	1.00
Total	$9.00

Figure 4.3 Intraday volatility

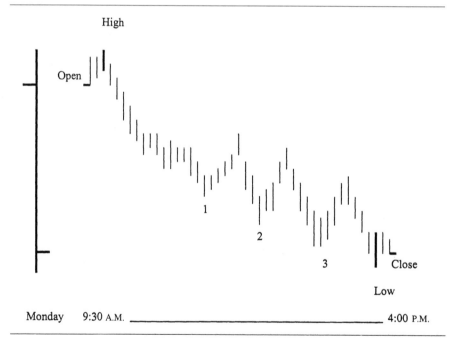

High

Open

1

2

3

Close

Low

Monday   9:30 A.M. _____ 4:00 P.M.

After you record this information, you simply divide the total by the five days. This tells you that the *average dollar price volatility* for the week is $1.80. Finding this average can be helpful to you as a day trader and a microtrend trader. Over time, you will come to know the aura of volatility that surrounds a specific stock and the average price range of this volatility.

Figure 4.3 illustrates the intraday trading range for a given day of the week. In this example, you see how day traders can go long or short during the day. Even though the trend was down for the day, there were three different occasions where a trader could have gone long during an intraday downtrend. These points are identified by the numbers 1, 2, and 3 in Figure 4.3. The highest probability for this given day would have been to go short after the open and remain short as long as possible. Instead of trying to scalp a fraction of a point, you are staying with trend as long as possible. When the trend reverses, you exit the trade. Electronic trading technology gives you the ability to enter and exit trades within seconds. Electronic trading technology will be addressed in Chapter 6. For now, just understand that this technology far exceeds that of online trading, which is conducted over the Internet.

The aura of volatility that surrounds all price movement must always be taken into consideration, especially when you are considering an intraday entry or exit and when placing a stop. If you are a microtrend trader, you will want to identify the high-low range—especially the lows. An excellent technique for placement of stops is to plot a moving average of the lows. You usually do not get stopped out by the high or the close of the day. It is the lows of the day that typically trigger a stop. Placing a stop on or slightly below a moving average of the lows when a stock is trending will typically keep you from being stopped out prematurely. Stop placement and other trading tactics will be covered in Chapter 5. Now that you understand the importance of identifying intraday volatility, let us examine what will become a very important part of your success: intraday bullish and bearish chart patterns.

High-Probability, Profitability Intraday Chart Patterns

One of the biggest mistakes I see traders make is overloading themselves with information. One of the keys to short-term trading—especially day trading—is to keep your analysis simple and clean. The analysis that leads to your individual stock selection will take time, but it is absolutely necessary. Once you have selected the stocks you are going to trade in real time, simplicity becomes the key. Your buy or sell decision must be quick and concise. One of these factors is your interpretation of real-time bar chart patterns. All of the chart patterns are based on *five-minute* bar charts, with a fifteen-minute chart used to confirm the trend.

The following series of real-time intraday chart patterns and explanations will guide you in your search for entry and exit points. With all patterns, remember to ask yourself, *What time is it?* Remember that the first two hours and last two and one-half hours of the trading day have the most volatility, though usually trending in one direction or another. This trending momentum, once identified, can be used in your favor. Remember, the center of the day is the grinder. I suggest you avoid it at all costs. Enter the grinder only if you are in a trade and that trade is still trending.

Bullish Chart Patterns

Look at Figure 4.4. Note at point A the rounded bottom and the steady trend up to resistance. At point B, you will see a breakout above resistance, with the close above the resistance line. Look for an improvement in a one-minute momentum indicator and possibly an increase in volume. If you enter at point B, you would place a stop at point C. If the uptrend reverses, it is likely to retest support. By placing your exit point below what has now become support at point C, your chances of not being stopped out prematurely are greatly improved. The longer the consolidation remains at resistance before the breakout the better. As a point of interest in real-time intraday chart work, you will find that, as a rule, the longer the price remains at consolidation before the breakout, the stronger the momentum of that breakout will be. The key is not to get impatient

Figure 4.4   Retest of resistance

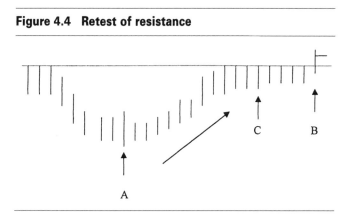

and make your move into the trade before the signal has occurred. Time and time again I have witnessed traders who are action addicts enter before the signal tells them to. The result is a loss on a perfectly good trade. The only reason the trade failed is because they were in a hurry. Successful traders are patient people—they let the trade come to them. Success in short-term trading means waiting and watching for the right moment. When it arrives, you take instant action, but until then you calmly watch and wait. A high-probability, profitability style of trading involves more concentration and thinking than the frantic outbursts typical of a scalper. Trading intraday trends is far more relaxed and enjoyable because the trend lasts longer and there is more profit potential in trading a trend than in trading increments of $\frac{1}{16}$ or $\frac{1}{8}$ of a point.

Figure 4.4 showed a retest of resistance. Let us look at a similar intraday chart pattern that you will see quite often. In fact, it is the first part of another pattern that most traders trade every day without realizing that two parts make up this pattern. The first part is the rise to meet resistance.

Take a look at Figure 4.5. Point A shows the rise of price to resistance. Note that resistance was penetrated slightly and then began to consolidate below resistance. This is an important factor for you to key in on. The arrow at point B shows a tight, narrow high-to-low price range. The *longer* the time frame of this range the better. There is a high probability of price breaking out above resistance. Do not enter the trade until the breakout occurs. You can lose

---

Figure 4.5   Rise to meet resistance

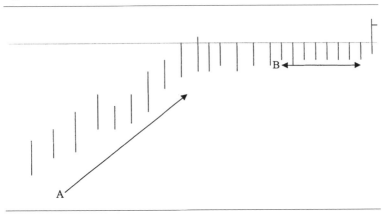

---

a lot of money by anticipating the trend and taking the trade early. Do not *guess* the direction of trend. When it reveals itself, then make your move and enter the trade. The rise to meet resistance is part of a high-probability chart pattern known as the *trending breakout of consolidation*. Do not confuse this pattern with an ascending triangle formation.

The rise to resistance many times is the first step to a trending breakout of consolidation. This is a very powerful and frequently seen intraday bullish chart pattern. It occurs in stocks that have strong trending potential. This pattern can last for a long period of time. It can rise several times and is a much safer pattern to trade than a price trend that shows a parabolic pattern. When a parabolic run occurs, you are expecting a retracement of price, which can be as much as 50 percent. But the trending breakout consolidates two or three times, allowing the bullish momentum to keep exploding upward without exhausting itself. Look at Figure 4.6. Point A and B show the breakout of consolidation. Also note the overall trend is up, as each consolidation is higher than the last. I have found this to be a very profitable chart pattern to trade. Remember two factors when trading this pattern. First, when price consolidates, be ready for a reversal to the downside, and second, watch the clock. It has been my experience that if this pattern enters the grinder (middle of the day), the consolidations have a much greater probability of

Figure 4.6 Trending breakout of consolidation

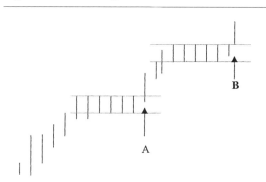

breaking down and not continuing upward. This price pattern is one of the longest of the bullish patterns and can continue for one or two hours. The average time for this pattern is between 30 and 45 minutes. Let us examine several other bullish intraday price patterns.

Ascending triangles work in real time when they are more *compressed.* Examine Figure 4.7. The letter A shows the breakout of the triangle formation to the upside. If the triangle is *not* compressed, then the resistance line will most likely hold and price will turn down. Always check momentum and look at the price lows. Ask yourself, Are the lows rising or beginning to trade lower? If they are rising, then there is a good probability that the price will break out to the upside.

At point B in Figure 4.7, note that the high-low range is starting to compress even further. This could indicate that momentum is beginning to slow down. At this point you must wait to see which way

Figure 4.7 Compressed ascending triangle

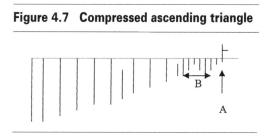

price will move. In daily price patterns, an ascending triangle is very bullish. This is not the case with intraday ascending triangles. The more compressed the triangle, the greater the upside breakout. If you do not have the compression, and if you see compression of the high-low range identified by letter B, this pattern will be bearish, *not* bullish. This information is contrary to what most traders believe to be true. The difference is in the detailed analysis of the pattern, which you now know and understand. From now on, when you see an intraday ascending triangle, do not just assume it is bullish until you examine the points I have outlined.

Figure 4.8 shows what the bullish pattern looks like. In a real-time five-minute chart, if the pattern is wider at the base than this, it will show strong resistance, and price will usually not break out without strong buying volume. The ascending triangle patterns that work best can be visually described as a wind sock or cone shape with a flat top. Figure 4.8 is a visual example of the shape I am describing.

Be careful not to mistake a tight consolidation pattern with a compressed triangle formation. Many times, new traders (and some times even experienced traders) will make this error. If you have any reservations, use the figures in this chapter to help you identify the correct price patterns. Do not guess. Guessing is hazardous to your wealth.

Extremely volatile stocks will have a massive sell-off once or twice during the trading day. This intraday sell-off can become an excellent point at which to *short* the stock, making this strong downward move a bullish trend you will want to take advantage of. When this trend begins to correct, a climax selling reversal can be played by taking a profit on your short position and, at the right moment, going *long* (buying the stock). The key to identifying this reversal of trend is a series of points I have outlined in Figure 4.9.

Figure 4.8   Bullish pattern

Figure 4.9   Climax selling reversal

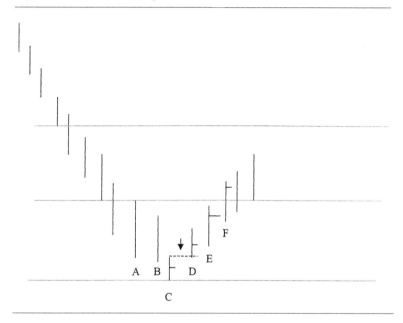

First you need a protracted downward sell-off intraday from an overbought condition. Then you need the following factors in the order in which I have identified them to occur. Price bars A and B show a slowing of a major sell-off. Note how the lows are closer together and the high-low range of bar B is less than that of bar A. Bar C shows a smaller high-low price range than price bar B. Point D shows price reversing direction. The important thing to note here is that the low of D is at the previous high of C. This is highlighted by the downward arrow pointing to the dotted line. This line is showing the high of bar C, which is equal to the low of bar D. The low and high of bar E are higher than the low and high of bar D. Another factor important to the continuation of the trend reversal: From bars C to F, the closes are higher and you begin to see a trend of higher highs and higher lows. I have traded this pattern many times and found it to be profitable. Most of the money comes from the short side of the trade. The long side usually will rise 20 to 30 percent of the decline, but it will typically take twice as long to rebound as it did to fall. This is because markets and stocks will generally fall 67 percent faster than they rise. The key to the reversal is understanding factors A through F. Once you know this information, you can add this pattern to your trading kit.

The oversold extreme reversal is a pattern that you will see many times. This pattern is especially prominent in technology stocks, which are prone to a large degree of speculation. This speculation results in massive volatility, and in most cases buying and selling reach points of extreme. The key to this pattern is identified by bars A and B in Figure 4.10. Bar A shows a large high-low range and a close toward the top part of the bar. Bar A is an extreme point of an oversold condition. If you remember basic statistics, think of bar A as being well outside the normal distribution of a set of numbers. Even though the trend is down, looking at Figure 4.10 you can see it is an extreme point. Bar A has an intraday close above the midline of the bar and toward the high of the bar. The midline is rep-

Figure 4.10   Oversold extreme reversal

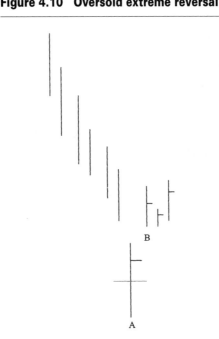

resented by the dotted line in Figure 4.10. Bar B is important in determining if the trend is reversing. Bar B is the very next bar, and it is above the high of bar A. Bar B is also trending higher and will have an intraday close toward the top of the range. In some cases you will have a gap up, as in Figure 4.10.

An open trend run is best described as a stock that has massive upward or downward momentum from the opening of the day. This momentum usually continues for 25 to 30 minutes. In most cases, the markets are also trending strongly in the direction of the stock. Identifying an open trend run begins with the first five-minute bar in Figure 4.11 (bar A). From the open, you have higher highs and higher lows. The lows stay above a 7- and a 17-period exponential moving average. You enter open trend runs early in the trend, using the low of the first opening bar as your exit point. When the stock begins to consolidate, or it puts in a parabolic run at the end of an extended move, you can take your profit. Letter B shows price starting to consolidate and lose momentum. This would be an excellent place to take your profit. You could draw a support line like the one in Figure 4.11, and if the stocks drop ⅛ or ¼ point below that support line on a five-minute bar, you sell. In some cases, the open trend run

Figure 4.11 Open trend run

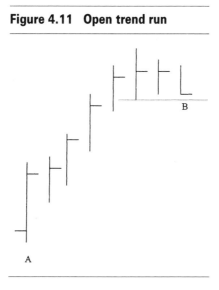

will turn into a consolidation and then trend higher. Once consolidation begins, momentum slows down and you have two decisions to make. Sell, or wait for momentum to resume and trend higher. If momentum does not resume, sell when it breaks the support line.

In Figure 4.12, day 4 shows the *inside day*. An inside day is inside the high and low range of day 3, and the dotted lines show this relationship. Once a stock begins to move, usually it will move for three to five days in one direction if the momentum is strong enough. A breakout above a 12-day exponential moving average with the close toward the high of the day is usually enough to drive the stock for three days or more. The fourth day is critical to the buy or sell decision. If the fourth day looks like it will close lower, then you will sell. This is especially true if the day opens with all the trading below the open, and the close in all probability will be at or near the low. If this is reversed, then the day 5 may be higher than day 3. If day 5 is a Friday, you should probably sell or place a stop at the low of day 4. Going into a weekend with a large position is never a good idea without placing a stop.

Figure 4.12   Five-day run with an inside day

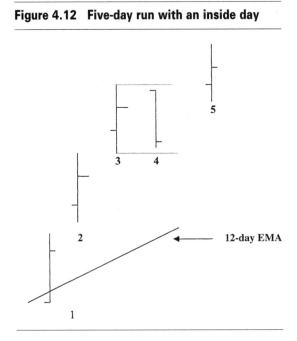

Bearish Chart Patterns

The pattern shown in Figure 4.13 forms after a long upward move in trend slows down. As momentum stalls, buying and selling create a consolidation pattern. This pattern will occur after an explosive opening. Remember Figure 4.11, the open trend run? Many times, the open trend run will become a consolidation exhaustion failure.

The double top formation is usually a high-probability, profitability chart pattern. (See Figure 4.14.) There are several factors that lead to trading the double top with a high-probability outcome. One of the most important is to concentrate on the word *top*. For a double top to become a bearish pattern, you must have a long, protracted run-up until you encounter resistance. Momentum stops and price begins the first downward move, identified by letter A in Figure 4.14. Price then moves to the neckline, identified by the dotted line at letter B, and rebounds back to retest resistance at A. Upward momentum fails, and once again price begins to fall to the neckline. Letter C shows price breaking below the neckline and moving lower. Once price moves below the neckline, you short the stock, placing a protective stop exit at letter D. The key to identifying a double top is focus on the word *top*. The pattern will fail if it does not have the necessary long, protracted run-up to make it a top formation.

Figure 4.13 Consolidation exhaustion failure

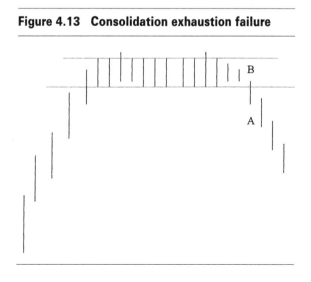

Figure 4.14   Double top

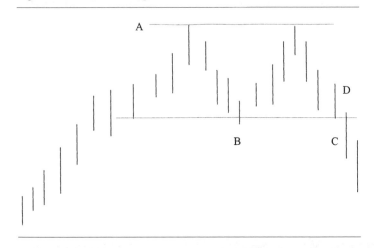

One of the most important patterns to learn to identify is parabolic run. A parabolic run is an angle that violates the normal angle of ascent. Usually, the angle is greater than 45 degrees. In Figure 4.15, the angle is identified by the dotted line. The arrow points to the reversal day when the last buyer came to buy at the high. From that point on, the trend was down in a sequence of lower highs and lower lows. Long parabolic moves downward are characterized by a long run-up in price at or near a top. Parabolic runs are important to identify because you typically do not want to buy stock right after a parabolic run occurs. Parabolic runs have two rules that you should always keep in mind:

1. When a parabolic run takes place, expect a retracement. This retracement can be 30 to 50 percent of the previous move, or the 17-period exponential moving average on a five-minute bar chart.
2. Once a parabolic move has taken place and a reversal day is in place, look for a consolidation to occur.

Parabolic runs and the rules that accompany them are true in daily and intraday bar chart analyses.

Figure 4.15   Parabolic run

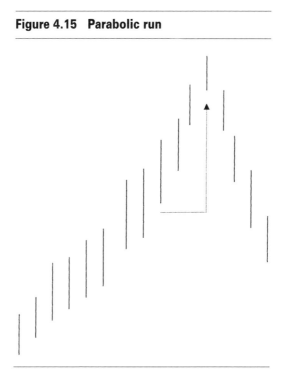

In many cases, chart pattern rules that hold true in the analysis of daily bar charts are inaccurate when it comes to intraday charts. An excellent example of this is an ascending triangle formation. In daily analysis, this chart pattern is very bullish and a very highly profitable pattern to trade. This is not the case with an intraday ascending triangle. Let's look at the example of an intraday ascending triangle in Figure 4.16.

Figure 4.16   Ascending triangle

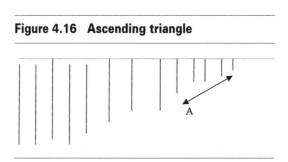

Letter A shows the range in a five-minute chart becoming smaller toward the apex of the ascending triangle. When you see this beginning to occur, the probability of a price breakout above the dotted resistance line is minimal. This pattern in a five-minute chart is bearish, not bullish—the opposite of what it would be in a daily chart. As always, you wait for confirmation of the price break. If the base at the far left of the chart pattern is wide, as it is in Figure 4.16, it is far more likely that the resistance line will hold, turning back any bullish breakout. If the base is narrow and price rises in a more even and normal fashion toward the apex of the triangle, it is likely to break out in a bullish trend above the resistance line. It is important to understand that an ascending triangle pattern is the opposite of the classic bullish pattern.

After a gap, the pattern forms a descending pennant with lower highs and lower lows, as shown in Figure 4.17. When price breaks down, it should travel lower by the distance measured from the widest part of the pennant to point A. Point B illustrates the downside projection. Pennants come in all sizes. The line drawing to the right in Figure 4.17 shows the basic form of the pennant. It can be a large or a

Figure 4.17   Descending pennant with a gap

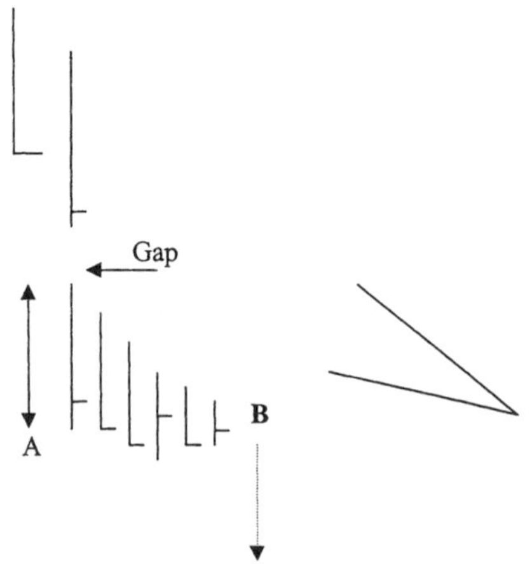

small formation. Pennants as a rule are not high-probability chart patterns. This particular chart pattern is one of the few that work out more than 50 percent of the time. Learning to identify intrachart patterns is critical to your success. Most new traders do not understand that bearish patterns can be far more profitable than bullish patterns. Let us now learn about intraday by shorting.

chapter 5

high-probability shorting

One of the most closely guarded secrets of electronic day trading is how to successfully short a stock intraday. Unfortunately, the information on this subject is almost nonexistent. Without the knowledge of how and when to short a stock intraday, success as a day trader or short-term trader will be much more difficult to achieve. Making money in downtrends is a completely foreign concept to the vast majority of people. Most people don't understand that you can make money faster when the stock market goes down than you can when it goes up. Not understanding how to make money in a strong downtrend seriously handicaps your ability to compound capital and limits your options. After all, the market doesn't always go up, does it? In fact, markets tend to drop an average 67 percent faster than they rise. The problem is that stocks tend to trend upward. To make money shorting, you have to know when a stock has a high probability of beginning its downtrend and where the downtrend is likely to reverse. To complicate matters further, you need to understand the long-term technical picture of a stock, the market, and the sector to make consistent high-probability intraday trades.

To become a success in shorting (or short selling) requires you to become a true master of the game. You must be in tune with the trend of the market and be able to use technical analysis to scrutinize the specific stock you plan to short. *You must know the fundamental picture of a company before you short it if you plan to hold the stock three days or more.* If you plan to hold a stock longer than one day, *never short on technical analysis alone.* An understanding of both fundamental and technical analysis is necessary if you are to be successful shorting stocks. I know of cases where traders went short because of technical analysis while holding stock overnight only to have to cover the short position a few days later for a large loss. If you are shorting stock intraday using ECNs (Electronic Communications Networks) and trading electronically, the fundamental picture is not as critical, because you plan to be out of the position before the end of the day. If you know of fundamental weakness, it makes the case for shorting the stock more compelling. Before we begin to examine the techniques of intraday shorting and trading electronically, let us first learn some basic information about selling short.

How Shorting Works

The profit potential from shorting is made when the stock goes down. Just as there are uptrends, there are downtrends. Once you find a stock in a downtrend, or if the price is extended, you have a potential short candidate. Specifically what to look for will be covered later. For now, let me explain the basics of shorting.

Suppose you think the price of XYZ stock is going to go down from its current price of $32. Most people would call a broker and tell him or her that they want to *sell short* 500 shares of XYZ stock. To short stock, you must have a margin account already in place. Your broker then *borrows* 500 shares of XYZ stock from an account and sells them to you. At once, $16,000 is deposited in your margin account. This cash earns interest, which will be discussed later. You might be thinking, "Wow, $16,000! I love this short selling stuff." Unfortunately, this is not the end result of short selling. Since you *borrowed* the stock, you will have to return it to your brokerage firm at a later date. The $16,000 is in fact borrowed money. Here is how you make a profit. If the stock drops to $25, you can buy back the 500 shares for $12,500, return the stock to your broker, and keep the profit of $3,500 minus the commission. The $3,500 is the difference between what you sold the stock for, $16,000, and what you bought it back for, $12,500 ($16,000 − $12,500 = $3,500). You may not quite understand yet that you made money without any initial cash outlay.

What if you are wrong and the stock price goes to $40? How could this happen? Because you were stubborn, saying to yourself, "It can't go any higher." The words *it can't* are not in any serious trader's vocabulary. Traders know that anything can happen, and they act accordingly. Always place a stop to cover your short position, just as you would when going long. If you are trading electronically, *you* are the stop. If the stock went to $40, you would have to pay $20,000 plus the commission to buy back the 500 shares. Ouch! In theory, going short has unlimited risk, because price could rise forever. Conversely, a stock can fall only to 0, having no value after that point. Because shorting involves unlimited risk, the SEC requires a margin call when losses reach a calculated amount.

Margin

To sell short, a broker will require you to put up minimum collateral of 50 percent of the value of the short position. If the collateral, less any unrealized losses, falls to 30 percent of the value of the original short position, or if the stock price rises so that the collateral minus losses equals only 30 percent of the short position, you will receive a *margin call.* This means you must add additional assets to bring the value of the collateral, less losses, back up to 50 percent of the short position or, alternatively, liquidate the account. Trick or treat. Don't worry. If you use common sense, you won't get a margin call. Margin used properly is the path to riches. Just don't get greedy; use it intelligently.

When you open a margin account, you must sign a *hypothecation agreement,* which says you will pledge your stocks as collateral against your loan. The *rehypothecation agreement* allows your broker to loan your stocks to a bank or to other customers. Rehypothecation is the pledging of the client's securities to secure loans from banks. In this way, securities firms can afford to carry margin accounts for their customers. Securities worth 140 percent of a client's debits is the legal maximum that may be rehypothecated.

Dividends

Because you borrowed the stock, any dividends that come from selling short belong to the broker who either owns the stock or has borrowed it. If you are going to hold short stock for more than a day, you need to find out if and when the dividends will be paid out. Many stocks that are good short candidates don't pay dividends. A large number of growth stocks with high P/E ratios fall into this category. If you day trade, you needn't worry about the dividends because you will be holding a trade only until the end of the day.

Uptick Rule

When you short stock you are subject to what is called the *uptick rule*. This means that you can't sell the stock short unless the most recent trade was higher than the *prior trade*. If the price was 56½, and the next tick in price was *any fraction* above the half, you can short. Another part of the uptick rule is known as a *zero-plus tick*. If the previous trade was 56½, and the next trade was 56⅑₆ followed immediately by another tick of 56⅑₆, you could short at 56⅑₆—a zero-plus tick. A zero-plus tick occurs when a trade takes place at the *same price* as the previous trade but at a higher price than the last different price. In this case, the stock ticked from 56½ to 56⅑₆, which is an uptick. If the tick is followed by another tick of the same price (56⅑₆), it is a zero-plus tick and you can short it. The uptick rule was instituted due to the role of short selling in the 1929 stock market crash. At that time there was no uptick rule and you could sell stock short at any price. Selling on a downtick exacerbated the decline. After the Crash of 1929, the uptick rule was adopted.

Hedging, Arbitrage, Hedge Funds, and You

It is estimated that 95 percent of short selling is a direct result of institutional hedging and arbitrage. Interestingly, hedge funds contributed only a small percentage to short selling. Shorting stock as a regular strategy to make money, other than in the case of arbitrage, is not normally practiced on Wall Street. Most of the time, fund traders buy the stock to go long with the intention of holding it overnight. When institutions enter a short position, they usually are held overnight as well. All of this information is important to you if you are planning to short on a regular basis.

Sometimes it is difficult to find stock to short. This is especially true on the Nasdaq if you are trying to short stock that has small trading volume and little liquidity. I would suggest that you not trade this kind of stock no matter what the hype. Most brokerages will have a *short list* of stocks that are in their inventory. If you are going to short a stock and hold it overnight, I suggest you have liquidity. Having stocks on this list usually means that the broker has enough on hand in case you have to cover a short position. If you are going to short, I suggest you short intraday and *not* hold a short position overnight. If you short intraday, you are short stock for only minutes or a few hours. By the end of the day you are out of the trade. Liquidity is almost never a problem for electronic traders who short stock during the day. Some electronic trading firms have a short list of stocks that you can check if need be. As an electronic trader you will find that you will be short almost as much as you are long. This being the case, you must learn to become a highly skilled short trader. Part of becoming a skilled short trader is understanding institutions and their behavior. Sometimes this behavior can lead to a short-covering rally.

Shorting Can Be Bullish

Institutions that take short *positions* (large number of shares)—a trader would call it *size*—at some point have to buy them back. This buying activity tends to drive up the stock price. You want to know what the short positions in the stock are like and whether there is a lot of put option activity as well. This information can be found in the short-interest section of *Investor's Business Daily* or the *Wall Street Journal*. This information is available on a monthly basis.

Short Interest and Put/Call Ratio

Short interest is the total of all shares sold short and not covered as of a specific date. In the old days, this was considered a good way to judge how bearish or bullish a stock looked. A high short-interest number is bullish and low short interest is bearish. This is not as useful as it once was because funds use short selling as an arbitrage technique. Short interest is also altered in conjunction with end-of-year tax strategies. You need to understand short interest and put/call ratios because a rally may take place. In this case, lots of bears are not good for your shorting strategy. The market always seems to swing to extremes and move away from those points in the opposite direction.

The Short Squeeze

As the price of the stock you shorted moves higher, you will be forced to exit your short position by buying back the stock. Once the Street recognizes that there are a lot of short positions in a given stock, traders might buy the stock in an attempt to drive up the price. When the shorts start covering their positions, the upward momentum can be tremendous. A frightened short seller will pay almost any price to get out of a stock. In most cases, a rally started by short covering will not last very long. This is the first short squeeze. Get ready to be squeezed again by a danger little known to short sellers called the *second squeeze.*

The Second Squeeze

The second squeeze can hurt you more than the first squeeze. This occurs when your broker needs to return to the lender the stock you borrowed. This can happen if the original lender needs to sell. The lender can be the brokerage firm, or, if it doesn't have the stock, the firm can borrow it from a client's account. The broker may not have additional shares to loan, in which case your stock will be returned. This is another reason to sell short stock intraday. You don't have to worry about the second squeeze because you hold the stock for only a short time or until the end of the day. You are not carrying the short position overnight and exposing yourself to market risk. If you do plan to carry a short position overnight, make absolutely sure that the stock is available for you to cover the position and place an exit stop.

Short List and Fundamental Factors

You will need to know before you short a stock if it is on your brokerage's short list. This is a list of stocks that the broker can allow you to short. Quite often, you cannot short a stock because the broker does not have it in inventory or can't get it for you. This can be a real problem. Do your homework before you waste a lot of time in analysis.

When you are planning to short a stock and hold it longer than one day, you need to know about the fundamental factors influencing that stock. Remember, you are looking for factors that lead to a decline of growth, which will lead to a decline in the stock price—just the opposite of what you would normally be looking for. Here is a list of the most important fundamental factors:

1. *Annual earnings growth.* Look for a company with a decline in the annual earnings growth rate. Consider a company that was growing at 20 to 50 percent and is now losing money and posting lower annual growth projections.

2. *Quarterly growth.* Following a news announcement calling for lower earning and lowering of analysts expectations, look for a decline in quarterly earnings growth.

3. *Management or company culture revision.* Look for a major change in management—if possible, a change in company culture that would be a radical departure from the current one.

4. *Institutional selling combined with insider selling.* Are funds selling the stock? If so, has the sector just moved out of favor? This would be very good for the short seller because *traders* holding the stock long would sell the stock to avoid a massive sell-off. Look for selling of stock by major executives, which may be a forewarning that they are in fear of losing their jobs and want to raise cash. This would have even more impact if it comes at the same time institutions are selling the stock.

5. *Debt and cash flow.* Is the company taking on debt or financing with the use of bonds? Is there a problem with the company that is expected to affect cash flow?

6. *New technology and competition.* A combination of technology and competition may place the company's future in question. This is usually brought to your attention by a news story or an analyst's report. Pay close attention to companies that only have one or two products and are vulnerable to other technology and competition.

7. *Sector change.* Look for companies that are in the top of their sector because, as the sector rotates, they usually will end up at the bottom. Sector analysis is one of the most important parts of your work. Knowing which three sectors are on top and at the bottom is key to your success in general.

8. *Take over or merger.* In some cases, a takeover of a company will cause the stock to drop because the takeover is perceived as not being in the best interests of the company or its stockholders. Likewise, a merger can have a negative effect on a company. *Be careful with this one.* Don't anticipate a negative impact until you are sure.

High-Profile Momentum Stocks

Be very careful about trying to short stocks that are on *everybody's buy list.* How many times have you heard someone say, "If Intel or Microsoft go down, I'm going to buy some." You go short at the exact time when the stock is considered by many to be a good buy. Caught in a short-term rally, you have to cover your short position, which only adds to the rally. For the most part, you should *avoid* shorting stocks like this unless you have an excellent understanding of the specific stock's support and resistance areas as well as its normal volatility.

If you are shorting using ECNs (Electronic Communications Networks), you will still need to know the stock's support and resistance levels. As with all buy and sell decisions, you will use technical indicators and technical analysis. Because electronic traders usually sell a stock short for only a few minutes or hours, fundamental factors will only help you identify a stock that should begin or stay in a bearish trend.

Electronic Shorting

The major problems with shorting come when you hold the stock overnight. When you short the stock intraday, the vast majority of problems with shorting vanish. In my humble opinion, shorting stock electronically intraday is the best way to short. If you are wrong on the direction, you still will lose money but you don't have the other problems that plague short sellers. You can also exit the trade, thus keeping your loss small.

Now that you have the basic information you need about the concepts of shorting, let us address the subject of shorting stock for short periods of time using ECNs (Electronic Communications Networks) to route our trades.

High-Probability Shorting Methodology

There are two strategies for shorting stocks that have a high-probability outcome. The first strategy is to find stocks that are extremely overbought. The second strategy is to find stocks that are at the beginning of or in an extended bearish trend. Both of these methodologies involve a screening process. Successful short-term trading generally is based on long-term analysis. When you are looking for stocks to short, you will use daily bar charts on one year of price data. Analysis of this time frame will reveal stocks with the highest potential to short. Our objective is to first find stocks that are in an extremely overbought condition and stocks that are entering an extended bearish trend. Let us examine this screening process.

Macroscreen

The following four points are part of the macroscreening process:

1. Identify the trends of the S&P 500 and the Nasdaq markets.
2. Identify three to five top sectors.
3. Identify five stocks in each of these sectors that exhibit the most overbought conditions.

4. Identify stocks in your own computer database that exhibit the most overbought conditions. This will be accomplished by using an overbought filter. This filter will enable you to scan your database on any given day in search of stocks that may soon become excellent candidates to short. My filter can be found in the MetaStock software from Equis International.

A very important point: Stocks that are overbought can remain in an uptrend for an extended period of time. After you have identified stocks that are overbought, you need to analyze each one for signs of potential bearish trend reversal. You are looking for microtrend and intraday candidates. Remember, not all stocks are equal when it comes to bearish potential.

Shorting Overbought Stocks

Step number one is to identify the trend of the markets at the time you are planning to short stock. For the best results, you will want a market that is extended. The more parabolic the uptrend the better. Another point you want to remember is the months that are the most bearish from a statistical basis: September and October. For example, if the month of August is bullish and the market index is at an old or a new high, be aware that a bearish trend has a high probability of occurring in September and October. Many times after a summer rally, a sell-off of stocks will occur from August into October. This is, of course, not always the case, but over the past 100 years September and October have had a bearish tendency.

Note in Figure 5.1 that the market is breaking above resistance and heading for an old high. At the same time you can see that September and October may possibly influence the current trend. Support and resistance are always important to any bullish or bearish analysis. The more parabolic the run over a short period of time, the higher the probability of a reversal of trend. Remember the parabolic rules from Chapter 4: (1) "When a parabolic run occurs, expect a pullback of 30 to 50 percent." (2) "If a pullback does not

Figure 5.1   Trend of the S&P 500
Chart courtesy of MetaStock®

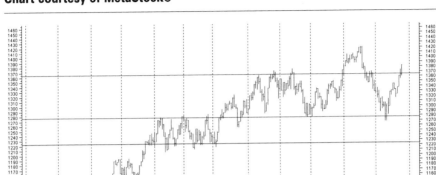

occur, expect a **consolidation**." In case you have forgotten, a parabolic run is a movement in price that violates the normal angle of ascent and is greater than 45 degrees. A parabolic run is almost vertical in nature. The parabolic rules are true for markets and for individual stocks. See the example of a parabolic run (Figure 4.15) in Chapter 4.

After reviewing the sectors and identifying individual stocks that appear to be overbought, make your selection. You will follow the stocks on this list until it is time to take action and short the stock. The following factors are necessary for successfully shorting overbought stocks.

1. Extended price trend
2. Parabolic run in price
3. Overbought technical readings on the following indicators:

RSI (14-day)

CCI (12-day)

Bollinger bands

Moving average (3-day) EMA of the close rolling over and changing the slope downward

MACD beginning to turn into a sell signal at price highs (least important of the technical factors)

These factors are important for the microtrend and the intraday trader. In fact, if a stock has these characteristics, it is an excellent candidate for intraday trading. Now that we know how to screen and select a stock that is overbought, let us begin to examine specific information that should improve your intraday trading.

Intraday Shorting of Overbought Stocks

"Short stock *intraday?* Shorting is risky enough as it is, and you want to short intraday?" This is the typical reaction of nonprofessionals. This response is based on emotion, not on knowledge or experience. To the layperson, it seems a risky venture, but the fact is that shorting intraday is safer in many ways than holding a short position for a long period of time. If you are using a shorting strategy, you need to know a few important pieces of information. If you examine trend direction you will find the bias of the stock market is upward. This upward bias has been the case for over 100 years and is not a modern statistical aberration. Because the bias of the market is, in fact, upward, your stocks will be candidates for shorting only 5 to 20 percent of the time. This means that on a percentage basis, you are usually long 95 to 80 percent of the time. When you look at intraday trend trading, the picture changes dramatically. Remember, on average, markets and stocks fall 67 percent faster than they rise, and in some cases price will drop 80 percent faster. This rapid drop can compound money at an unbelievable rate. Trading the downtrend of a stock is essential for success in the market, and nowhere else is this more obvious than in intraday trading.

Intraday shorting is subject to rapid and volatile changes in trend. This is due to traders trading different time frames on an intraday basis as well as other factors that contribute to momentum. You can be the beneficiary of this intraday volatility by knowing when to short. When you examine the intraday bias of stocks, they tend to be 40 percent bullish, 40 percent bearish, and in consolidation 20 percent of the time. As an intraday trend trader, you *do not* trade consolidations. This means that when you trade intraday, you are long 50 percent of the time and short 50 percent of the time. The 50 percent of the time you are short has the potential to compound money 67 to 80 percent faster than trading the long side of intraday trend.

When you are looking for intraday overbought conditions, you will be using 5- and 15-minute bar charts. The 15-minute chart confirms the trend and break of the 5-minute chart. You are looking for a stock that has an extended chart pattern and, if possible, a parabolic run for the last one to three bars. Figure 5.2 is an example of a possible intraday trend that is ready to begin a bearish intraday decline.

Figure 5.3 shows a 15-minute chart of the same stock and confirms the current trend of the 5-minute chart. You can use the 5- and 15-minute charts to approximate the turning point of a stock that is overbought and parabolic. Often the 15-minute chart will show you a chart pattern, such as a symmetrical or ascending triangles, that may not be as well defined in a 5-minute intraday chart. I will give you an example of this from an actual real-time trading experience. I was following Lucent Technologies, symbol LU, and the 5-minute

Figure 5.2 Overbought intraday stock
Used with permission of Townsend Analytics, Ltd.

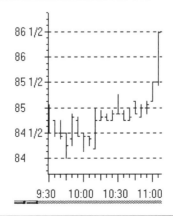

Figure 5.3   Fifteen-minute intraday chart
Used with permission of Townsend Analytics, Ltd.

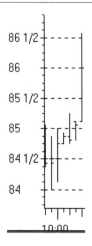

chart was in a <u>high-low trading range</u> and was hitting what at the time was resistance at $68. It broke through resistance and moved to $68⁵⁄₁₆, then fell back to $68. I was going to go long the stock, when I glanced at the 15-minute chart. Clicking on a trend-drawing tool, I drew a line connecting the lower upward-moving lows of the trend. I realized that the 15-minute chart showed the formation of a symmetrical triangle and that we could be near the apex of that triangle. My first instinct was to go long from $68, expecting a breakout above resistance to $68½. That is exactly what I would have done if I had not had the 15-minute to confirm the trend and pattern. Ten minutes later, the stock broke through the apex of the triangle and moved downward throughout the rest of the day.

Fifteen-minute charts do not always show chart patterns, but when they do, you need to pay attention. Not doing so could cost you a lot of money. The 15-minute chart will show trend direction and trading range. You base your buy and sell decisions on the 5-minute chart. This time frame tends to give signals that are less distorted by speculation. When you trade intraday, you need to have 5-minute, and 15-minute, and daily charts showing at least three months of daily price information. See the example of a 15-minute intraday chart in Figure 5.3.

Another reason for considering an intraday short position would be a strong downtrend in the major markets. If the markets are topping out or beginning to decline, in most cases your stock will follow. If you are trading stocks on the Nasdaq and you are watching only the S&P 500, this could be financially fatal. Many times, markets will trade independent of each other. I suggest that you follow the S&P 500 *and* the Nasdaq markets. Have these markets charted on your computer screen so you can monitor them at a glance. Figures 5.4 and 5.5 show five-minute charts of the S&P 500 and the Nasdaq markets. (In Chapter 8, the details of setting up a trading room will be addressed, including screen configuration, hardware, monitor array, and other information.)

In both charts you see the intraday trend moves of the markets. This becomes important in your timing decision to go short or long, because most of the time you want the market to be in sync with the direction of your trade.

Electronic Shorting Using ECNs and Level II

When you short a stock while trading electronically, you have control over risk that no other form of trading can give you. If you are

Figure 5.4   Intraday five-minute S&P 500
Used with permission of Townsend Analytics, Ltd.

Figure 5.5   Intraday five-minute Nasdaq
Used with permission of Townsend Analytics, Ltd.

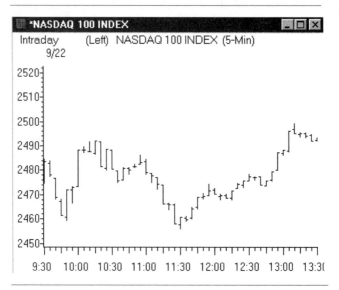

going to short or use leverage of any kind, you need to be able to manage the risk of the trade. In my opinion, this is the most important advantage of electronic trading. You click your mouse and two to six seconds later your bought or sold confirmation is on the screen. As I have said before, trading online through an Internet brokerage firm is *not* going to give you the risk control you need to trade intraday. You need the speed and reliability of being able to route your order over the proper ECN at the price you select. Because you are trading electronically using ECNs and Level II market maker screens, you have the necessary information to short the stock and control the risk. Here is an example of how to use this information to sell short intraday.

The S&P 500 and Nasdaq are beginning to top out and the stock you have targeted to short has run parabolic for the last 15 minutes. You feel very confident that the market and the stock will begin an intraday downtrend. Wanting to sell short, you look at the Level II market maker box and here is what you see.

Selling Short Reading Level II

BID ↑	ASK
NITE 23⅝	SCWD 23¾
GSCO 23⁹⁄₁₆	ISLD 23¾

The bid is currently an uptick expressed by the up arrow to the side of the bid. NITE is currently bidding at 23⅝ and GSCO at 23⁹⁄₁₆. Given the following positions of market makers NITE, GSCO, SCWD, and the ECN ISLD, here are several ways to short XYZ stock. Assuming that the ⅝ is an uptick, you could hit NITE at ⅝ by routing the order through the Small Order Execution System (SOES). In this specific case, you would want to use a *SOES limit order,* not a SOES market order, the reason being that if NITE *drops the bid* after filling a previous SOES order, it will cancel your order and you will not be able to hit GSCO at ⁹⁄₁₆. *You cannot SOES a market on a downtick.* If the bid had several market makers present at ⅝ and the market showed an uptick, you could use a SOES market order. Always remember to check the *size* (number of shares) on the bid and ask before you place any trade. With several market makers at ⅝, you would have enough supply to fill your short order. The probability of all market makers dropping at the same time before you filled your short would be slim. It could happen, but the odds are in your favor.

The market maker SCWD is on the offer (ask), offering stock at $23¾. If you wanted to sell short on the offer (ask), you could join SCWD, routing your order through Island (ISLD) and short at $23¾.

In the following example, Island (ISLD), an ECN, is at 23⅝ on the bid, and market maker Goldman Sachs (GSCO) is at 23¹¹⁄₁₆ on the offer (ask). If the bid is an *uptick,* then you can hit ISLD, selling short and routing through ISLD, but if the bid is a *downtick,* then you join GSCO on the offer (ask) at ¹¹⁄₁₆ on ISLD. Remember, you cannot hit ISLD on a downtick, you cannot SOES selling short on market downticks, and you cannot SOES an ECN.

BID ↑↓	ASK
ISLD 23⅝	GSCO 23¹¹⁄₁₆
	ISLD 23¹¹⁄₁₆

The previous examples have shown various ways of using Level II information to sell stock short intraday. To make money from intraday shorting, you are going to have to buy back the stock to profit from the trade. Sometimes a novice or even an intermediate-level trader will become confused by shorting. Old habits die hard, and it is easy to make a mistake because shorting is the opposite of what you normally do. When you short, your first step is to *sell* the stock, the opposite of buying. To take your profit on the stock, you *buy* it back. *When shorting, you sell to buy and buy to sell.* Here are several examples of *covering* (buying back stock) to take your profit. Do not confuse this with the term *short covering,* which usually is synonymous with buying back the stock at a loss to protect yourself from the stock moving higher. Let's look at several examples of how to use Level II information and how best to route your order.

In the following example, NITE, a market maker, is on the bid at $30⅝. INCA, an institutional ECN, is at $30¹¹⁄₁₆, followed by market maker GSCO at $30¾. You cannot use a SOES market order because INCA is an ECN, and, as you know, you cannot SOES an ECN. The best way to buy back your stock and take a profit in this specific example is to use the ECN Archipelago, known by the symbol TNTO or ARCA. By routing the order on Archipelago, you are able to hit INCA at ¹¹⁄₁₆. If INCA lifts the offer, your order will then hit market maker GSCO at ¾.

Covering Short Reading Level II

BID	ASK
NITE 30⅝	INCA 30¹¹⁄₁₆
	GSCO 30¾

You might be thinking, "If I can use Archipelago to hit an ECN and a market maker, this would be the best routing choice." If you did, it would be a serious error that could cost you thousands of dollars. Archipelago (TNTO) has what is known as SelectNet preference. This means that an order coming in through TNTO gives it 20 seconds to acknowledge, and it does not have to fill your order until then. A lot can happen in 20 seconds. Archipelago can be effectively used to hit ECNs in specific situations that appear during a trading day. Let's look at some specific examples.

The following example shows how to use Archipelago to cover your short position. MASH, a market maker, is on the bid at $28⅝. REDI and BRUT, ECNs, are on the offer (ask) at $28¹¹⁄₁₆. You want to buy back 1,000 shares to take a profit on your short position. In this case, you use TNTO to hit both ECNs: REDI for 500 shares and BRUT for the balance. This would be far better than trying to use SOES to hit GSCO for the full 1,000 shares. This trade also puts time on your side because by using TNTO to hit the ECNs you will be in front of the SOES crowd trying to hit the GSCO.

BID	ASK
MASH 28⅝	REDI 28¹¹⁄₁₆ 500
	BRUT 28¹¹⁄₁₆ 700
	GSCO 28¾ 1000

The following is another example of how you could use TNTO to your advantage. ISLD is at the bid at 40⅝, showing 1,700 shares. On the offer (ask) ISLD, GSCO, and INCA are at 40¹¹⁄₁₆. All are showing various numbers of shares they are offering out for sale. If you had to buy 2,000, you would use TNTO. You might be able to get the full 1,000 shares from ISLD, but if GSCO is in a 17-second refresh from being hit by a SOES trader, you could lose your opportunity. By routing the order through TNTO, you can be more certain of being totally filled with the 2,000 shares. If you had to fill only 1,000 shares or less, the preferred and fastest way to route would be ISLD, SOES, and then TNTO.

BID		ASK	
ISLD 40⅝	1700	ISLD 40¹¹⁄₁₆	1000
		GSCO 40¹¹⁄₁₆	1000
		INCA 40¹¹⁄₁₆	2000

Let us take a look at another situation that comes along quite often. Many times, the spread on the bid and the ask is very small; in rare cases, they will both show the same price. In some cases, you may, in fact, want to cover the position on the bid and not the offer (ask).

BID		ASK	
ISLD 33⅝	1700	GSCO 33¹¹⁄₁₆	1000

ISLD is on the bid at 33⅝ with 1,700 shares, and GSCO is on the offer (ask) at 33¹¹⁄₁₆ with 1,000 shares showing. If you want to cover your short position quickly and fill 1,000 shares, you need to buy back on the *bid*. If ISLD is showing 1,700 shares, you can feel reasonably confident of getting the full 1,000 shares, because ISLD has no refresh policy. That is not the case with GSCO. Once GSCO has filled 100 shares of a previous SOES order, it has 17 seconds to refresh before it accepts the next order. If your order arrives during the 17-second refresh, you may not get your price or the number of shares you need. In this case, it is in your best interests to sell at a lower price. Being greedy and trying to make that last dime is financially dangerous. I have known individuals who have lost thousands of dollars trying to get that last ⅛ of a point. This little personality flaw is a ticking time bomb. Acknowledge the problem and *correct it* before your account blows up and you become another notch on a faster trader's gun.

Understanding how to use Level II information and how to route the order is critical to all short-term traders, especially day traders. This technology is light-years beyond trading online. In most cases, your trade is transacted is seconds and the confirmation is on your screen before an online trader can type two symbols. It is my opinion that in five years most online brokerage firms will shift from their current methods to the use of ECNs. Why would anyone want to use traditional online methods when they can have the speed and power of trading like market makers?

Shorting at the Wrong Time

Before we move into an in-depth analysis of shorting tactics, we need to answer the question, "Why do most individuals short at the wrong time?" The first thing you need to understand is that individuals for the most part do not short stock. Professionals do most of the shorting, and it is usually related to hedging a portfolio. When individuals do short, timing and analysis do not seem to be factors in the decision process. It appears that they short stock from an emotional reaction rather than as a strategy. I have examined thousands of short trades made by individuals. Here is a brief scenario of my observation on shorting.

The typical mistake that individuals make when they short is jumping in too late in the downtrend. In many cases, the trend may have lasted for a month or two. About this time, a news event comes out on XYZ company and catches the attention of Sam Novice. Because the news is negative, Sam assumes that no one is going to buy this stock and that most people are going to be net sellers of the stock. *Wrong!* This same event becomes the catalyst for a reversal in the downtrend. Value fund managers have had their collective eyes on XYZ stock for some time. The news caused the stock to move just a few points lower. Now the stock is down almost 50 percent and value fund investors feel compelled to buy the stock because they believe it is "cheap." About the same time, several astute technical analysts see that XYZ is at a long-term support area and in a Fibonacci retracement zone. Other analysts notice that the stock is in a pivot zone where rebounds have taken place before. Big money is getting ready to go long two days after Sam shorted the stock. In Figure 5.6, the arrow at point A shows where Sam shorted the stock and the arrow at point B shows where big money is getting ready to go long.

Figure 5.6   The wrong time to short
Chart courtesy of MetaStock®

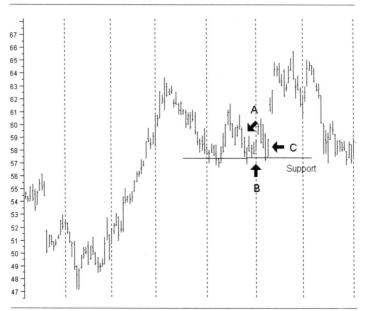

In this example, Sam would have been much better off shorting if the support area did not hold. He could have placed his stop above support, identified by the arrow at point C.

In the second scenario, Sam has been watching a stock for a few weeks and decides that it is excessively high. What is he basing his decision on? He simply has a hunch that the price is "just too darn high." So Sam shorts the stock. Sam knows nothing about topping patterns or technical indicators; he just reasons that no one is going to pay higher prices for that particular stock. Sam helps the stock move even higher because he is forced to cover the stock. One month later the stock is just starting to consolidate after moving higher.

In Figure 5.7, the arrow at point A shows where Sam went short. Never make the mistake of arbitrarily deciding the stock or a market is too high without data to support your contention.

Figure 5.7   Long trend run
Chart courtesy of MetaStock®

Short Trading Tactics

Here are a few important bits of information you need to know when you are trading intraday.

1. Intraday trends that move strongly in one direction usually last 5, 15, 20, and 35 minutes. One intraday trend out of thirty will last for one hour or more. $1/30 = 1 \text{ hr}$

2. Gap breakouts of intraday chart patterns tend to move in the direction of the breakout, lasting on average from 5 to 20 minutes.

3. End-of-day trend tends to continue into the first 10 minutes of the next trading day.

4. Lower closes and lower lows project the probability of lower prices 85 to 88 percent of the time. This trend usually lasts for three days before reversing.

5. Markets and stocks have a three-day cycle.

6. The first 2 hours and the last 2½ hours of the trading day exhibit the most stable and identifiable trend.

7. Sector rotation may be identified by heavy intraday selling in the last 45 minutes of the trading day. Weeks later, these stocks show up on the most-active list.

By studying the following examples, you can focus on the fine points of shorting overbought stocks. After studying overbought stocks, we will turn our focus to the second high-probability selection, which is finding stocks that are at the beginning of or in an extended bearish trend that is unlikely to reverse for some time.

Figure 5.8 shows a chart of Hewlett-Packard. The bars reflect daily data over a one-year period of time. Remember, you begin your search for overbought stocks by using daily price data. Let us begin our analysis of the chart.

1. The first step is to look at two years of past history for support and resistance as well as other information that will give you an idea of the stock's personality. Every stock has a personality. It reflects the traders who are trading the stock and what they are likely to do at certain prices. You will notice that Hewlett-Packard has a habit of putting in one-day reversals after long runs in trend. When the trend reverses, the stock falls several points very quickly. These runs occur after a breakout of price above a 12-day exponential moving average of the close. After this occurs, one and a half to two months later, a one-day reversal takes place at a high. In most cases, just before the one-day reversal a parabolic run has occurred. (See Chapter 4 to review parabolic runs and the parabolic rules.)

2. After examining the trend reversals, you note that volume tends to exhibit spikes at these highs. This is not usually the case for most stocks, but it is part of Hewlett-Packard's personality. This information gives you further clues for establishing a high-probability shorting point on the stock.

3. After plotting several technical indicators, it becomes obvious that when an RSI (14-day) has a reading of 75, the stock has a high probability of trending downward to the 12- or 50-day exponential moving average. The Moving Average Convergence/Divergence (MACD) indicator tends to exhibit sharp points just before the nine-day trigger line gives a sell signal.

This stock has all of the necessary components to be a highly successful stock to short. For the highest probability, you would want to short only at specific overbought points in time. Even though you are going to short intraday, these points give you the highest probability of success. They also exhibit the highest probability for the microtrend trader to short this stock. In all short-term trading, timing

Figure 5.8   Hewlett-Packard parabolic and overbought
Chart courtesy of MetaStock®

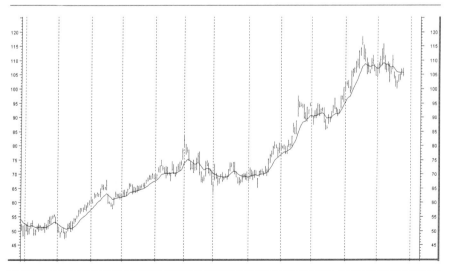

is everything. Shorting is a technique that demands high skill and superb timing. Before we look further into shorting tactics, let's take a closer look at Figure 5.8 by examining the information in points 1 to 3.

In Figure 5.9 you will see long trend runs marked by trendlines. At the end of each of the marked trends you will note a one-day reversal, which is indicated by a circle around the reversal day. As you know, this is a bearish signal. When you combine the one-day reversal

Figure 5.9   Two years of history reveal personality
Chart courtesy of MetaStock®

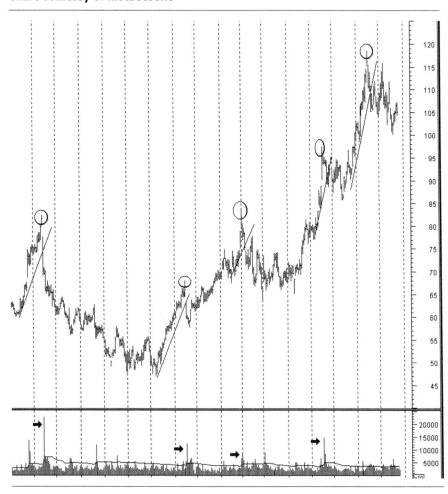

with a parabolic run-up, you have a high probability of trend reversing. When this trend does reverse, in most cases it will fall to the 12-day EMA or the first support level. This is important to know because it is at this point that you might want to cover your short position and take a profit. Figures 5.10 and 5.11 show a one-year time frame.

In Figure 5.10, you can see the one-day reversal, parabolic runs, the 12-day EMA, and the 1½- to 2-month trend cycle. Note that when price closes above the 12-day EMA, trend begins to move and continues for 1½ to 2 months. The cycle is identified by the numbers at the bottom of the chart. When you plot moving averages, make sure

Figure 5.10   Hewlett-Packard one-year chart
Chart courtesy of MetaStock®

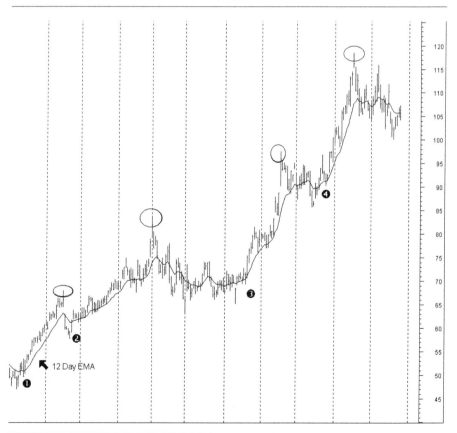

Figure 5.11   Hewlett-Packard
Chart courtesy of MetaStock®

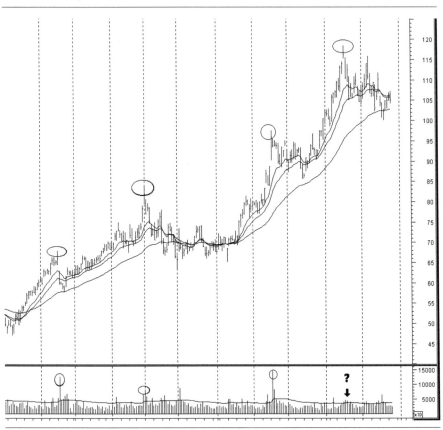

that you know where the 12-, 20-, and 50-day EMAs are on the chart in relation to price. This information is of extreme importance because price tends to rebound from these moving averages a very high percentage of the time.

In Figure 5.11, note the volume spikes that are circled in the volume histogram. Volume information is not always a true indicator of the price trend. Many times, volume will remain flat or below average, giving *no* clue as to accumulation or distribution. In this case, Hewlett-Packard announces its intentions and repeats its behavior over and over again. Superior traders pay attention to the personality of each stock they trade—and are usually rewarded for their observations.

Figure 5.12 shows two technical indicators. Both RSI and MACD indicate an overbought condition that is ready for a reversal in trend. When the Relative Strength Index (RSI) has a reading of 75 or more, the stock is extremely overbought. The arrows identify these points on the indicator. The standard overbought reading for RSI is

Figure 5.12   Hewlett-Packard and technical indicators
Chart courtesy of MetaStock®

70, identified by the line across the top of the indicator. A reading of 75 exceeds the standard overbought reading, which is the default for most trading software. I have always found it necessary to plot the RSI indicator on one year of data for this very reason. By looking at the data, you can usually find a more accurate overbought reading based on the price behavior of the stock. In this case, 75 is a more precise reading and is identified by the number 2 line at the top of the indicator.

The Moving Average Convergence/Divergence (MACD) indicator comes to a point just before the nine-day trigger line renders a sell signal. MACD tends to be a little late with sell signals, but you need this delay for a true trend to develop. The turning points are identified by the arrow on the MACD indicator. Other indicators—CCI (12-day), Bollinger bands, and moving averages—are also used in your analysis.

All of this information is taken into account when studying the personality of a specific stock. All stocks have personalities that can give you a tremendous amount of information to help you decide whether to buy, sell, or hold, and which strategy would work best at a given point in time.

You have now identified an overbought stock and high-probability points at which to go short. Let us begin further analysis on a microlevel and identify possible intraday behavior of a stock.

Microanalysis

Microanalysis begins by studying the three-day exponential moving average of the close. The moving average is plotted with one year of daily data on the specific stock you wish to analyze. This specific moving average is extremely important to the short-term trader. In stocks and markets there is a 2½-day cycle of trend. This moving average identifies the short-term trend of the stock you are analyzing. By analyzing the three-day EMA you can refine your entry and exit points on a short-term basis. Let us take a look at several examples of how to use the three-day EMA.

EMA

...ng the three-day EMA
is ... d. In Figure 5.13, I
have plotted the ... As you look at
the chart, you not only ... he moving average. This helps you determi... rend. You will also
notice that when the three-day ... ge tops, it tends to
exhibit either a sharply rounded po... arp inverted V. This is
a pattern that short sellers will be looki... for, especially when the
top formation corresponds with a primary bearish chart pattern.
Bottoms tend to be slightly more rounded in shape unless the bottom is part of a reversal day spike. This is another positive feature of
the three-day EMA. It tends to trace out and make major chart patterns much easier to see. Yet another use of the three-day EMA is in
the placement of stops or exit points. This will be examined later in
this chapter. Let's identify the main features of the three-day EMA on
one year of price data before we take a closer look at microanalysis.

**Figure 5.13   Three-day EMA, Micron Technologies
Chart courtesy of MetaStock®**

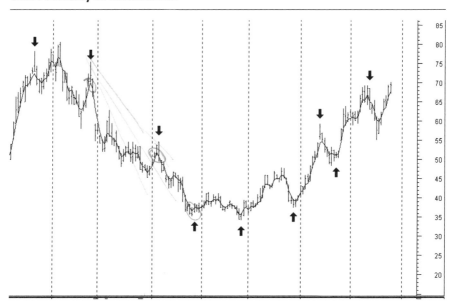

Three-Day EMA Features

1. Defines trend direction
2. Shows strength of trend
3. Confirms high points and low points by shape of the moving average (slope)
4. Confirms major chart patterns, making them easier to see
5. Assists in the placement of short-term stops or exits

Now let us examine the use of the three-day EMA on a microlevel. In Figure 5.14, you see the three-day EMA over a three-month period of time. One of the important points to note when looking at this chart is the relative position of the *close* above and below the three-day EMA. In most cases of trending stocks, if you intend to go long, the stock you will want to see will have closes above the moving average. When you are planning to short, you look for a topping formation and for closes to be lower on the daily price bar or below the moving average.

The three-day EMA can be used to place stops in two ways. First, you can use the three-day EMA to confirm long and short parabolic stop and reversal (SAR) points. Figure 5.15 shows how well

Figure 5.14 Three-day EMA microtrend analysis
Chart courtesy of MetaStock®

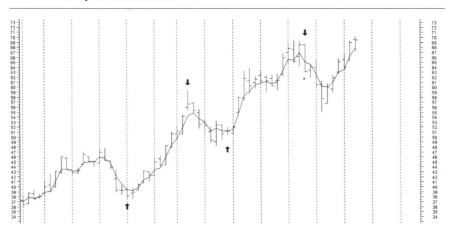

Figure 5.15 Parabolic SAR and three-day EMA
Chart courtesy of MetaStock®

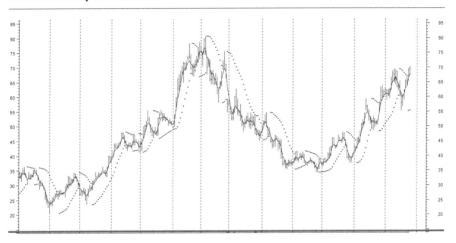

the two work together to keep you in the current long and short trend. The dotted points represent the suggested stop placement for parabolic SAR. The solid dark line represents the three-day EMA. Note that this chart covers one year of daily high, low, open, and close information for Micron Technologies.

Currently, Disney (symbol DIS) is not typically a volatile momentum stock. This is a perfect test of the three-day moving average stop placement methodology. Figure 5.16 shows a period of price consolidation in June, a decline into August, followed by an uptrend and a sell-off into August 31. In June, you see how the dark three-day EMA rounds out at the bottoms and results in sharp points at tops. When the stock trends, the same signature tends to repeat itself. This signature addresses the momentum at tops and bottoms and gives you an excellent idea of the direction of the trend and its strength. High-probability, profitability traders do not usually trade consolidation areas. They wait until a trend develops. In early July, the third top in the consolidation formed and then began a strong downtrend. Note that the dotted 12-day EMA is above the 3-day EMA. When you are short, you can use the 12-day EMA to place your exit stops. There are only two rules. First, cover your short position when the 12-day EMA crosses under the 3-day EMA.

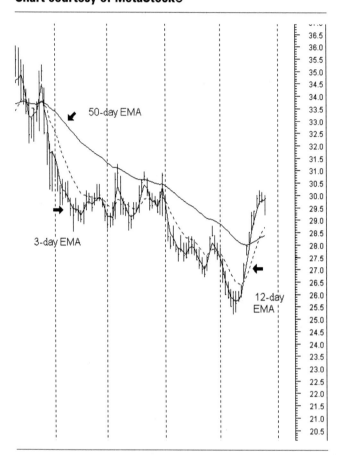

Second, cover your position when the close is above the 12-day EMA. Figure 5.16 also shows the 50-day EMA on the chart, which identifies intermediate trend. You will note that the trend has for most of this time period been bearish. Using the 50-day EMA in combination with the 12- and 3-day EMAs gives you a better picture of the major trend and whether it is bullish or bearish.

At the end of July 27, a top forms, and the next day price closes below the intersection of the 3- and 12-day EMAs. From that point on until a bottom is formed, the closes are toward the low of the daily price bar and below the three-day EMA. On August 10, the close begins to reverse, closing above the three-day EMA and alerting you to a possible change in trend. August 13 shows a break above the 3- and 12-day EMAs, with the close above the 12-day EMA. If you were still short, you would cover your position at this point and take your profit.

Microtrend Bearish Patterns

I use the word *pattern* in the context that patterns tend to repeat themselves. The examples are intraday bars of usually only 15 to 30 minutes' duration. If you use them in combination with the intraday bearish patterns in Chapter 4, you should have excellent results spotting intraday shorting opportunities.

Intraday Trend Spike
This occurs when you have an explosive bullish move. It appears to work best when the momentum begins after the open and continues for an hour or more. The last three or four 5-minute bars show large intraday high-low range. At point A in Figure 5.17, the price has

Figure 5.17 Intraday trend spike

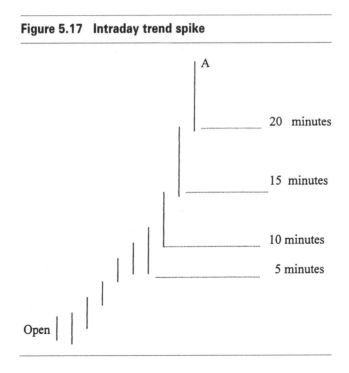

...distance of three 5-minute bars—in this case, to the low of the price bar marked 10 minutes. When using this technique, it is a good idea to know the average price range for the stock on bullish days. At point A, look for the market to begin showing signs of weakness. While you still have an uptick, short the stock. Figure 5.17 gives you a visual image of what an intraday trend spike trend looks like. Knowing the stock's personality is important, and this comes with time and experience. You will see this pattern over and over again.

Intraday Bearish Trends

Identifying intraday bearish trends is important in order to gauge the strength of the trend and estimate how far it will move. You know that bearish trends tend to decline 67 to 80 percent faster than they rise. A bearish trend that will sustain a long bearish move over time has specific characteristics. These bearish characteristics are seen in Figure 5.18, which shows the following:

1. There are three bars or more of lower lows and lower highs.
2. The close on the bar is near the low or below the middle of the bar.
3. The lows and highs form excellent declining trendlines.
4. At least three bars in the trend have larger high-low ranges.
5. Price angle of descent is contained within the lows of the line formed by the three major bars.
6. The closes of the three major bars are consecutively lower.

Intraday Exhaustion

After a run in trend of 30 minutes, the five-minute bars will tend to exhibit a smaller high-low range and begin to stall trend. This is represented by the letter A in Figure 5.19. Watch this area very closely because it may signal an intraday shorting opportunity. The last three or four price bars should have the appearance of shrinking. This is a result of reduction in the high-low range as seen at the top of Figure 5.19. Another key to this pattern is that the first three or four

Figure 5.18   Bearish trend

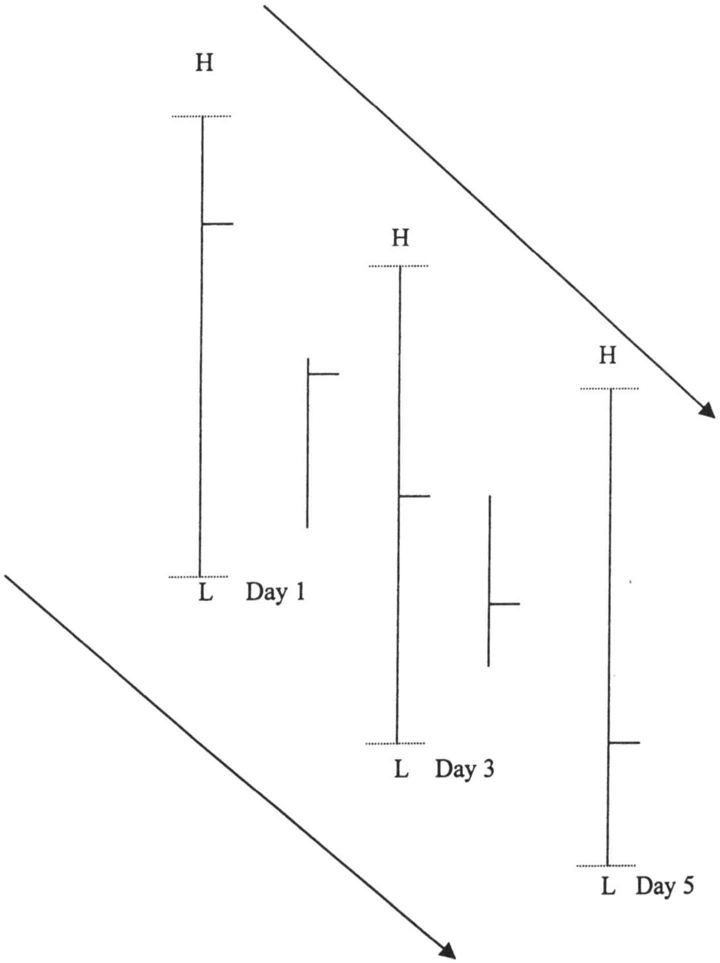

bars should have higher highs and higher lows. This is represented by the price bars between the dotted lines indicated by letter B.

We have examined the information on overbought conditions that relate to microtrends and intraday shorting. You have learned screening procedures useful for the day trader and microtrend trader. Now let us turn our analysis to the long term by defining bearish long-term trends and discussing how we short them.

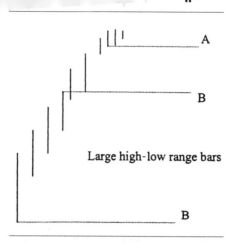

Large high-low range bars

Shorting Long-Term Bearish Trends

When selling short in downtrends, you have to be very aware of several factors that could cause a stock to rebound to old highs. The first thing you need to learn is how to identify when a stock is beginning to enter a bearish trend. Most of the time, you will see poor fundamentals accompanied by bearish chart patterns. Let me repeat something I have said before: *You do not short merely for technical reasons* when you are shorting a stock for three days or longer. You must have a poor fundamental outlook for earnings if the bearish trend is to last for a prolonged amount of time. Technical factors will help you enter the trade and will help you stay in the bearish trend until it is likely to reverse.

Bearish Technical Analysis

In analyzing a stock to short long term you are looking for a stock that has just entered a bearish trend or one that is currently in a bearish trend. Let's examine the major technical factors in the following examples.

Figure 5.20 shows a chart of Barnes & Noble from March to September. Fundamental information on the stock was negative at this time. By May 19, it becomes obvious that a bearish descending tri-

Figure 5.20   Bearish long-term analysis, Barnes & Noble
Chart courtesy of MetaStock®

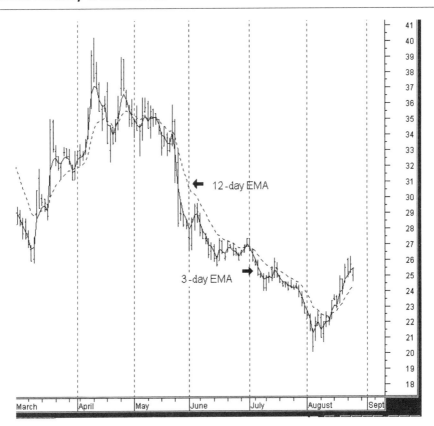

angle formation was in place. The 3-day EMA had put in a top on April 26 and moved below the 12-day EMA. The very next day, the 12-day EMA began to move lower. The lower trendline of the triangle was broken on May 21. From that point on, the price remained below the 12-day EMA until a short-term rally occurred on August 13. The arrow identifies the beginning of the long-term short entry point. The next two days gave you time to enter the trade and sell short. Using the 12-day EMA and the 50-day EMA to gauge trend direction and strength, it becomes obvious that this is a strong bearish trend that should last for a considerable amount of time. Because Barnes & Noble has liquidity, and the shares are readily

...the stock.

Upon examining the technical indicators, the case for shorting the stock becomes even more compelling, as shown in Figure 5.21. On April 29, the Moving Average Convergence/Divergence (MACD)

Figure 5.21   Technical indicators
Chart courtesy of MetaStock®

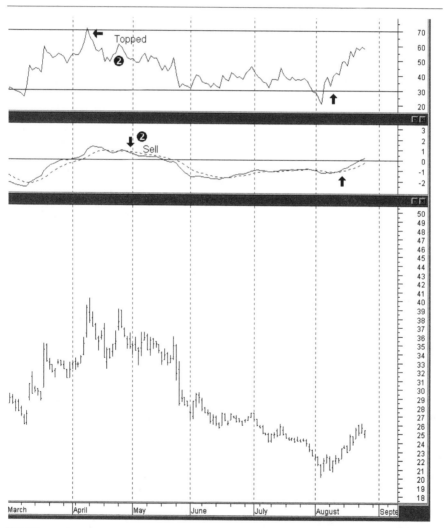

indicator renders a second, more powerful *sell* signal, identified by the number 2 on the MACD indicator (see Figure 5.21). A sell signal is indicated when the dotted trigger line crosses above the solid MACD line. Note that the slope of the MACD line is in a downtrend, with the second sell signal being lower than the first. The 14-day

Figure 5.22   Price rate of change, Barnes & Noble
Chart courtesy of MetaStock®

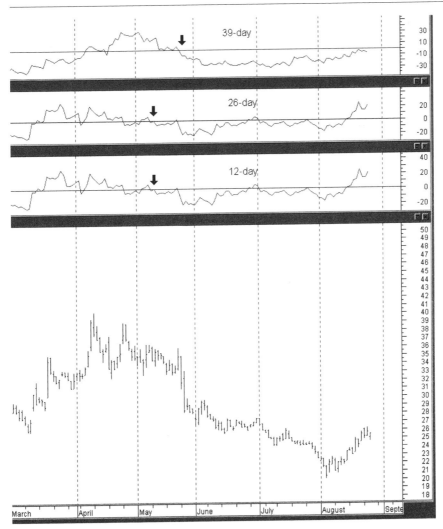

Relative Strength Index (RSI 14) topped out with a reading of 71.36 on April 9. This is indicated by the first arrow on the RSI indicator in April and the *topped* notation. From that date, RSI began to move lower. On April 29, when MACD gave its second sell signal, RSI put in a lower high and began to move lower. This is identified by the number 2 on the RSI indicator, which is above MACD. RSI remained weak for months, until the beginning of August. Both charts are marked with arrows indicating the signal.

Figure 5.22 shows 12-, 26-, and 39-day price rates of change for Barnes & Noble. Note that all three indicators are trending down. This is indicated by the downward trendline marked on all three ROC charts. Also note that price breaks below the support line on the descending triangle. The 12- and 26-day price rates of change are below the zero line. This indicates that both short-term and intermediate trends are bearish. On the following day, the long-term 39-day ROC indicator renders a bearish long-term sell signal.

chapter 6

electronic trading tactics

Webster's defines the word *tactics* as "the action part of a plan," "the science and art of disposing and maneuvering forces in combat," and "the art or skill of employing available means to accomplish an end." All three definitions apply to trading and aggressive investing. When you shorten the time frame of trading, you automatically pit yourself against the best traders in the world. Day trading and microtrend trading can only be described as war.

Most battles are won or lost in the preparation stage, long before the first shot is fired. It is important to anticipate your opponent's actions and reactions. Trading is high-tech warfare. Your opponent is a well-armed, seasoned, battle-hardened veteran of many campaigns. *Never underestimate* your opponents. Learn from them. If you hope to defeat a superior opponent, you must use cunning and superior tactics to emerge the victor. Why do so many traders and day trading cowboys insist on shooting from the hip? Yes, you might get lucky one or two times, but in the end it is the marksman who knows and understands tactics and the art of war who consistently hits the target. Remember, if you are not the marksman you are the target. You must be the general—the commander of your money. Each time you place a trade you are marching into battle. Winning generals protect their soldiers and commit them only when the probability of success is high. If the battle begins to go against them, winning generals pull out their soldiers to fight another day. How can you identify superior financial generals? They consistently make money and protect their capital by cutting losses quickly. In the following pages, you will learn the preparation and execution of electronic trading tactics.

One If by Land, Two If by Sea

The market is trending, the market is trending! You know from Chapter 3 that you must quantify the trend direction, duration, and strength of the markets before you consider a trade. All things being equal, you want the most dynamic trend possible when you place a trade. Some day traders will say, "Every day is a trading day. I will just follow the trend of the moment. If it moves, I will trade it." That trader will not be around three months from now because every day is *not* a high-probability trading day. When the market is strong and the stock you selected from your screening methodology is trending, it is time to trade. Market analysis and momentum screening is the way a general surveys the prospective battlefield and selects where and when to fight. Superior generals would not endanger their troops without gathering as much information as possible about the field of battle.

After you have ascertained the trend of the market and checked the sector performance, you analyze the trend of the stocks from your screens. Do not forget to consider the reward-to-risk ratio: You need a 2.5 or better ratio for the stock to be acceptable. If the trend score and the high-probability score are favorable, then identifying a momentum acceleration breakout is highly likely. If the stock has a 2.5 reward-to-risk-ratio based on daily price bars, you have a stock that has the potential to reward you on an intraday basis with points instead of fractions. Now let us look at various tactics and battle plans using electronic trading technology. Superior generals learn to fight the battles of the future from tactics and methodologies learned from the past. If you can learn from the mistakes of others and not repeat them, you have learned one of the most valuable lessons in life and in trading.

Time Cycle Correlation and Trading

One of the characteristics that successful short-term traders share is an understanding of time cycles and periodicity. An intraday trader should know the most statistically favorable bullish and bearish times to trade. For example, on an annual basis, November, December, and January are typically the most bullish months of the year. Conversely, the most bearish months of the year tend to be September and October, followed by February and June. If a strong bear market is in progress, it will tend to end in October. Bear market trends that begin in February or March tend to end in June. In some cases, summer rallies tend to end in June. Always know where you are in the annual cycle. Identify whether you are in a statistically bullish or bearish month. Of course, these rules of thumb do not always hold true, but annual cycles typically manifest themselves over and over again.

The best-performing days of the week tend to be Monday, Wednesday, and Friday. Currently, these days seem to have the most bullish tendency and tend to trend strongly. Another interesting and potentially profitable bit of statistical information is that the most bullish days in a given month tend to be the first three days and the last four days of the month.

The time periods that exhibit the most definable trends on the S&P 500 and the Dow Jones are 9:30 to 11:00 A.M. EST and 2:30 to 4:00 P.M. EST. Of particular importance are the last 45 minutes of the trading day. It is during this time frame that trend will either reverse or continue trending in the direction of the previous hour.

Extended Hours and 24-Hour Trading

The ECNs have fired the shot that will truly revolutionize how individuals trade around the world. Beginning with extended hours and then moving to full 24-hour trading, individual traders will have access to markets around the clock. This will change the statistical information you have just learned. Over time, as 24-hour trading by the public becomes more prominent, a new statistical field of information will be created. Twenty-four-hour trading will mean that volatility never stops. Investors will be *forced* by volatility to become short-term traders. Mutual funds will have far more volatility than they do today. Open-end, mutual funds that calculate the net asset value (NAV) at the end of the day will show large price fluctuations. These large swings in NAV will add to investors' anxiety. The old buy-and-hold strategies of past will create psychological stress. Investing will actually have more risk than trading because while you sleep your stock will still be in play. You may go to sleep with your stock up $5, feeling very good about the gain and sleeping well. However, in the morning, you may find that your $5 gain has become a $15 loss due to overnight trading. Investing as you know it today will be forever altered, and you will tell your grandchildren about the "old days" when people used to buy and hold. This change will cause the typical investor to become more actively involved in the management of his or her capital. Those who simply cannot handle the psychological stress will seek out a new breed of professional trader to manage their money, or they'll choose some other investment vehicles. The genie is out of the bottle. Nothing can put it back. These economic forces will not be restrained. Like it or not, 24-hour trading and ENCs are here to stay. They will become the new economic engines of all industrialized nations, adding to the liquidity of their markets. The ECNs will enhance the globalization of markets and bring the world closer together.

International trading will become a reality for the individual as a result of ECNs and 24-hour trading. Foreign stock traders will be able to trade U.S. stocks, and U.S. citizens will be able to trade foreign stocks at any time of the day or night. For the first time in history, *individuals* will create world markets, internationally linked by the ECNs. International and offshore trading capital will flow into the new 24-hour markets, adding liquidity as well as volatility. In these new and exciting markets, competition will cause the spreads on stocks to become smaller and smaller. This is in the public's best interest. We are already seeing the spreads on stocks becoming smaller on both the NYSE and the Nasdaq markets. This is a direct result of traders using the ECNs.

The Intraday Battle Begins

After quantifying the market trend direction, duration, and strength and identifying the stocks you are going to trade from your filtering screens, you are ready for the trading day. Remember, you are looking for only three to five of the highest-probability trades in a trading day. You want a trend to develop that will sustain for 15 minutes or longer, and for this reason an intraday trend trader usually will not enter the market at the opening bell. You want to wait until some form of trend establishes itself. In most cases, an intraday trend trader will wait a minimum of 10 minutes or longer before placing a trade either long or short. Let us examine intraday trading and tactics from a high-probability perspective.

Intraday Charts and Tactics

One of the very first things you want to identify is whether the stock you are following is in sync with the market or if it is trading counter to the market. Countertrending stocks will many times trend in sync with the major markets in the last 45 minutes of the day. This information is especially important if you short an intraday trend. If you are prepared for a reversal in trend you are less likely to be caught off guard than someone who has no knowledge of this stock behavior. Learning the personalities of stocks that you trade on a regular basis is very important. In Chapter 3, we discussed a strategy called "25 old friends." If you know the behavior of 25 stocks, you will have a feel for the length of the trend, support and resistance areas, average high-low intraday range, and whether the stock is currently trending with the market or countertrending. This knowledge will translate into confidence when it comes time to pull the buy or sell trigger. Most stocks especially, high-tech stocks, move in sync with the Nasdaq and the S&P 500. For this reason, the trend and relative technical position of the market is of the utmost importance in making a buy or sell decision. The time frame in which you view a stock or a market intraday is critical to entry or exit success.

Five-Minute Bar Charts

I have found over many years of trading that a five-minute bar chart gives me the best view of intraday trend, chart patterns, and support and resistance. If you trade a time frame that is less than five minutes, you are too close to the aura of volatility that surrounds the stock. If your strategy is to trade intraday trends, your objective is to identify and stay with the trend without getting taken out by the normal volatility of the stock. People who trade two-minute charts are, in fact, too close to normal volatility and are taken out of the trade too early. Another reason you, as an intraday trader, do not want to use two-minute charts is that institutions trade in this time frame. You cannot afford the commissions, slippage, and series of losses that trading in this time frame will give you. Most individuals mistakenly think they need to be as close to the beginning of the price move as possible. What you really want is to ride an intraday trend as long as possible. You will never be able to do this if you are too close to the stick (price bar), because the market makers will cause you to sell the stock by making you think the price is going down. Using a five-minute chart will put you just far enough out in time to establish solid intraday trend. When a five-minute chart reverses, it tends to be a true intraday reversal. Chart patterns that form in a five-minute chart tend to be very reliable and easy to trade. You learned about intraday chart patterns in Chapter 4. A five-minute chart will become your best friend, keeping you in trend and confirming entry and exit points.

Fifteen-Minute and Daily Bar Charts

You will use a 15-minute bar chart to confirm the trend and, in some cases, patterns in five-minute charts. Anything beyond 15 minutes is too far removed from the volatility of the stock to be of any real use to an intraday trend trader. By using a combination of the 5-minute and 15-minute charts, you gain a more accurate picture of trend, trading range, support and resistance, and momentum strength. I also suggest that you display a daily chart showing at least three months or more of data. This keeps you focused on the long-term trend. It also helps you maintain your sanity when a stock is volatile and you need to be focused on the major trend. Lack of focus on the major trend is one of the biggest problems with short-term traders. Never forget that your success will depend on identifying the major tend of the stock you are trading. This is true for all traders and aggressive investors. We all live or die depending on the direction and strength of trend.

The trading day begins with a look at the trend direction of the markets. I suggest that you use a five-minute chart, because you want your stock charts and the market charts to be in sync. This will quickly alert you to a stock that is trading countertrend. If you examine the chart of the S&P 500 in Figure 6.1, you will see a strong uptrend that continued all day. As you see in Figure 6.2, the Nasdaq matched the S&P with a strong uptrend. If you have selected a stock that has a high correlation to the movement of the S&P or the Nasdaq you would want to enter the trade intraday when the index is trending as it is in this example. I suggest you display the S&P 500, the Nasdaq, and, if possible, the Dow Jones Industrials on one of your computer monitors. This will enable you to determine the trend of the markets at a glance. Think of the indices as magnets that attract and repel stocks. This is a force you want to be in sync with. At the same time you are looking at major indices, you will

Figure 6.1 Five-minute chart of S&P 500
Used with permission of Townsend Analytics, Ltd.

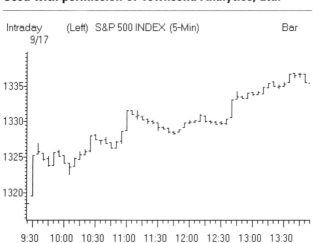

Figure 6.2   Five-minute chart on the Nasdaq
Used with permission of Townsend Analytics, Ltd.

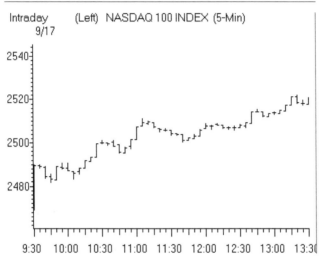

---

want to identify whether one sector is more active than another. The screening and selection process you ran the night before should identify sectors that are in play. The first 10 to 15 minutes of the market day should reveal the opening trend and whether the sectors you identified are in play. Do *not* buy in on the open because you have no idea of the true strength or direction of trend. I do not care what the futures are telling you. I have witnessed more money lost by traders trying to "jump the open" than by anything else. Do not be lured into this traders trap. Wait until you get a fix on the trend and only then enter the trade. There is nothing more demoralizing than starting off your day with a huge loss. Remember, you are *not* a gambler; you are a high-probability trader. Let the scalpers become demoralized and whipsawed on the open.

Many times, the S&P 500 and the Nasdaq will trend in different directions. You want to identify these times as well as the times they are trending in sync with each other. When they are in sync, as shown in Figures 6.1 and 6.2, finding a stock that has a sustainable trend is usually not difficult. Strong-trending broad-market rallies are one of the things that a high-probability trader looks for. Let us examine the technical factors in the following two high-probability trades. The first trade we will examine is shown in Figure 6.3, Intel Corp., which is traded on the Nasdaq.

The Nasdaq and Intel were in a consolidation pattern. At the same time, the S&P 500 opened higher and then began to trend lower until about 10:15 A.M. At 10:20 A.M. the Nasdaq market began to trend higher, and Intel broke through its trading range. The S&P 500 also began trending higher. At this point, both markets were in an intraday uptrend, with Intel moving higher as well. The five-minute chart showed that Intel had broken out of its trading range and was now trending higher. One of the techniques used by a high-probability trader is to look to the 15-minute chart to confirm the trend of the 5-minute chart. The 15-minute chart clearly showed that Intel was breaking out of a small, wide-based symmetrical triangle formation. This formation was not evident in a five-minute time frame. The 15-minute bar of the breakout had a high-low range that was equal to the first bar of the triangle. This was very bullish and was followed by another 15-minute bar that had a higher high and a higher low. The 15-minute chart confirmed the bullish breakout of the 5-minute chart. This bullish uptrend became parabolic 25 minutes after it began, and 10 minutes later it began to reverse.

**Figure 6.3   Five-minute chart of Intel Corp.
Used with permission of Townsend Analytics, Ltd.**

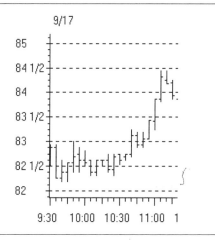

Remember that on average a strong bullish trend will move in one direction for 20 to 35 minutes, in some cases for one hour. This intraday trade was profitable, as Intel moved from an entry at $82%₁₆ to an exit at $84⅛. Later we will discuss the use of the one-minute momentum indicator in the entry and exit process.

Figure 6.4 shows the 15-minute chart of Intel Corporation. Note the parabolic run and the lost momentum.

About the same time, in another market, Motorola was moving in sync with the bullish trend that began the market day. The five-minute chart in Figure 6.5 shows Motorola moving from $89¼ to $90⅝ in 25 minutes and reversing at that point. The price run was of an extreme parabolic nature. Again, the 15-minute chart confirms the 5-minute chart and shows the upward advance of the stock beginning to slow. At the same time, the S&P 500 is moving higher, but Motorola is not advancing in price, and the one-minute momentum is becoming very bearish, showing a large volume of selling by traders. The decision is based on price action to sell the stock at $90¼. Figure 6.5 shows the 5-minute chart on Motorola, and Figure 6.6 shows the confirmation of the 15-minute chart.

Figure 6.4   Fifteen-minute chart on Intel
Used with permission of Townsend Analytics, Ltd.

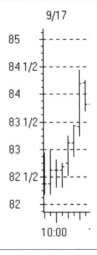

Figure 6.5   Five-minute chart of Motorola
Used with permission of Townsend Analytics, Ltd.

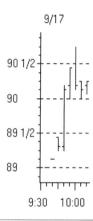

One-Minute Momentum

I find it very useful to create a separate one-minute momentum indicator of each chart that I am watching in real time. A one-minute momentum indicator chart will tend to smooth out the volatility and errors in tick data. Traders who trade using tick charts need to

Figure 6.6   Fifteen-minute chart of Motorola
Used with permission of Townsend Analytics, Ltd.

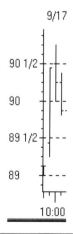

understand that tick data can be late and incorrect. The analogy I give my students is "If you trade too close to the fire you are going to get burned." By using the one-minute momentum indicator chart, you will gain a better picture of the short-term microtrend close to the stick (price bar) without suffering third-degree burns.

In Figure 6.7, you will see a one-minute momentum indicator of Intel showing price on the top and the indicator on the bottom. Notice how Intel's short-term momentum is gaining strength with higher highs in the indicator. Also note that Intel does not stay below the zero line for any extended period of time. At 11:15 A.M. the Nasdaq begins a downturn. Prior to this, the one-minute momentum begins to turn down from what was the third highest point of short-term momentum of the day. With this and other information, a decision is made to sell Intel. Here is the information that led to the sell decision:

Figure 6.7 One-minute momentum indicator and price of Intel

Used with permission of Townsend Analytics, Ltd.

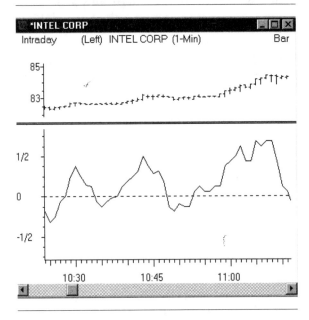

1. The Nasdaq market is beginning a downturn.

2. Intel has been in a bullish intraday trend for over 20 minutes.

3. Intel is now parabolic on both the 5- and 15-minute charts.

4. The five-minute chart is showing lower highs and lower lows.

5. The one-minute indicator shows momentum turning down from its highest point at that time.

Figure 6.8 shows the steady increase in price momentum until just prior to 10:00 A.M. At this time, the one-minute momentum indicator began a sharp decline. The 5- and 15-minute charts confirmed a parabolic price run and showed signs of slowing momentum that could lead to a reversal. In the case of Intel and Motorola, the one-minute momentum indicator of price aided in the buy and sell decisions.

Figure 6.8   One-minute momentum indicator and price of Motorola
Used with permission of Townsend Analytics, Ltd.

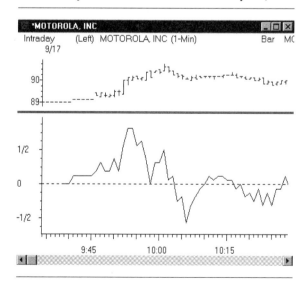

Moving Average on the Tick

If you feel compelled to use tick charts, I suggest using a moving average to smooth the data and errors. Using a 17-period exponential moving average of the close will help identify trend. I find this moving average to be very useful when timing an entry and exit decision.

Moving Averages and Periods

In previous chapters, you were shown how to use specific moving averages. Now we need to identify and discuss how to use them intraday. A moving average is, in fact, trend and can be used in both long- and short-term analysis of a stock or market. In most cases, you will use an exponential moving average, which gives more weight to the newer data. In previous chapters we used the 50- and 12-day exponential moving average to stay with trend. When you trade intraday, there are two exponential moving averages that look and act like the 50- and 12-day exponential moving averages. These are the 7- and the 17-period exponential moving averages of the close. These two moving averages are to be used *only on a five-minute bar chart.* When price is above the 7-period moving average it tends to trend for longer periods of time. When price moves below the 7 period exponential average it tends to stop at the 17. If the 17-period does not hold, the price will fall to the next support area. The 7-period measures short-term trend and the 17-period measures the intermediate trend, just as the 12-day and the 50-day moving averages apply to longer-term analysis. You can use the two moving averages to keep you in trend both long and short. If price moves above the 7- and 17-day averages, you are long, and if price drops below the 7-day average, you might consider shorting. Figure 6.9 shows how the two moving averages are used to stay short in a downtrend.

In Figure 6.9, the moving average line closest to the price bar is the 7 and the one farthest away or far above price is the 17. From the open of the day, the stock was in a bearish trend, moving below both the 7- and the 17-period exponential moving average within 10 minutes of the open and staying below them for 50 minutes. As long

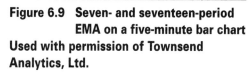

Figure 6.9   Seven- and seventeen-period
EMA on a five-minute bar chart
Used with permission of Townsend
Analytics, Ltd.

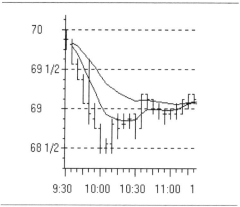

as price stays below the two moving averages, the intraday trend is bearish. Note that at 10:00 A.M. the price stabilized and did not fall further. Ten minutes later, price began to rebound off of $68½, rising to $69 and beginning to consolidate. Later in the day, around noon, the price broke out of consolidation to $69⅐₆. In both cases, price moves above and below the 7- and 17-period moving average. I have used these moving averages successfully for over 12 years. The key is to use them in conjunction with a five-minute bar chart. If you attempt to use them in any other time frame, you will not get the same result.

Figure 6.10 shows the 7- and 17-period exponential moving average of a five-minute bar chart. Remember that the 7-period moving average is the one closest to price and the 17 is furthest away. As price moves out of a consolidation and begins to strongly trend, you can see the value of both moving averages. They not only show the direction but the strength of the trend. As long as price holds above the 17-period average, the trend is strong. If it holds above both, you have a trend that will carry you much higher. This is a perfect example of how screening a stock and using intraday

**Figure 6.10   Seven- and seventeen-period EMA on a
five-minute bar chart on Micron
Used with permission of Townsend Analytics, Ltd.**

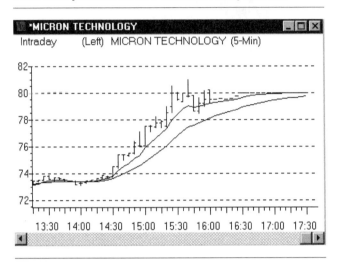

trend trading tactics capture points instead of fractions. This is typical of the type of trade a high-probability trader will enter, and it shows why this strategy is superior to scalping. Micron Technology gave only *one* high-probability buy signal all day, but you could have made more than three points on one trade. Remember, the best trends for intraday trading occur in the first two hours of the day and the last two and a half hours of the day. As you examine Figure 6.10, note how the two moving averages keep you in the stock as it trends intraday. There is simply no reason to abandon this trade unless it penetrates the seven-period exponential moving average. Use the violation of the moving average as a sell signal when the trend looks like this one and when it occurs at the end of the day.

Electronic trading tactics from a high-probability perspective are much more relaxed and focused than the frantic tactics of scalping. High-probability traders are looking for only three to five trades a day, staying with the trend until it ends. They use technical analysis and screening procedures to find high-probability trades, and then they use technology to control the risk of each trade.

Trading the Super DOT

Your Level II screen will show you the bid and ask prices of stock on the various exchanges. Remember that price improvement is possible on the NYSE because of the specialist involvement in the trade. If volume is good and the spread is wide, you can come in and buy on the bid and sell on the ask. For example, if the price is 79¼ on the bid and 79½ on the ask, you place a limit order to buy on the bid at 79¼. There is size (number of shares) on the bid, so you do not have to worry about your limit order. If you get filled and there is enough size on the ask, you can turn around and offer the stock out at $79½. Selling 1,000 shares, you pocket the spread minus the commission. Wide spreads do not always occur, so you have to be ready to act very quickly. If the ask price drops, you have to hit the Cancel button to cancel the trade. You could also buy high, becoming at that moment the best bid in the country. Once you are filled, you offer the stock out at the higher price. You would do this if you felt very certain that the ask price was going to move higher. I trade this way less than 5 percent of the time simply because I find trading intraday trends to be much more profitable and less risky. Figure 6.11 shows a Level II screen of the NYSE and the example just described.

In Figure 6.11, you see the routing set for ISI. This will route the trade to the Super DOT system. This system is not as fast as using and ECNs or SOES. An order will typically take from 3 to 6 seconds to be filled and in some cases up to 12 seconds. This is critical to remember because when you cancel a trade the electronic pulse may not get to the floor before your trade is filled. For this reason, you need to be very aware of the trend strength of the stock and the size on both the bid and the ask. As you see from this example, you are offering out stock at $79½ and capturing the spread.

One of the advantages of the setting speed is the potential for price improvement when you buy and sell stocks on the NYSE. I estimate that I get price improvement on limit orders 30 percent of the time. Another advantage of the Super DOT system is that it is very simple to use. If you are routing an order to the Nasdaq, you do not know if a market maker or an ECN is going to be at the bid or the ask. With the Super DOT you just buy or sell from a single screen with

Figure 6.11 Level II screen on NYSE, Micron Technology
Used with permission of Townsend Analytics, Ltd.

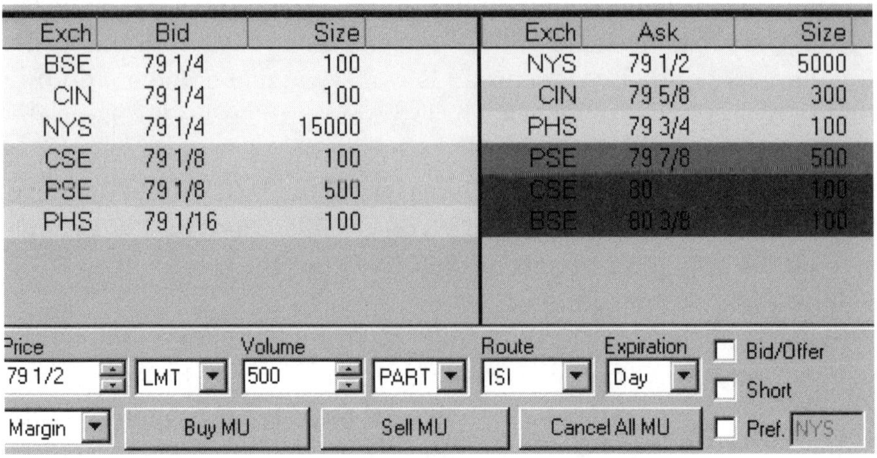

Exch	Bid	Size	Exch	Ask	Size
BSE	79 1/4	100	NYS	79 1/2	5000
CIN	79 1/4	100	CIN	79 5/8	300
NYS	79 1/4	15000	PHS	79 3/4	100
CSE	79 1/8	100	PSE	79 7/8	500
PSE	79 1/8	500	CSE	80	100
PHS	79 1/16	100	BSE	80 3/8	100

Price		Volume		Route		Expiration		☐ Bid/Offer
79 1/2		LMT ▼	500	PART ▼	ISI ▼	Day ▼		☐ Short
Margin ▼		Buy MU		Sell MU		Cancel All MU		☐ Pref. NYS

out having to set up a second screen. This simplicity makes the initial trade on the Super DOT very fast. After the number of shares is entered, then it is simply a matter of clicking the mouse on the buy or sell button. Nasdaq Level II order routing is not that simple for the reasons I described. I will show you a trick for fast order routing on the Nasdaq. This trick demonstrates the necessity for a multimonitor system. I suggest three or four monitors—two would be the absolute minimum.

Two Guns Are Better Than One
Say you bought 1,000 shares of stock and trend is beginning to slow down and may quite possibly reverse. It is time to sell. If you are trading the Nasdaq market electronically, you will need to use this tactic to expedite selling the stock. If you want to sell into the active market you will need to set up two different screens of the same stock. Because you do not know whether a market maker or an ECN is going to be on the bid or the ask, you must be ready to hit either one. If you remember from Chapter 2, you cannot SOES an ECN, and Island (ISLD) has no size or time restriction. Knowing this information, you set up the selling screen shown in Figure 6.12.

Figure 6.12 Selling screen, Level II
Used with permission of Townsend Analytics, Ltd.

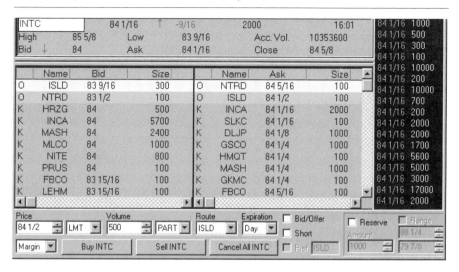

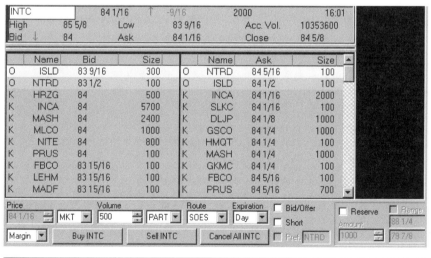

Both order-routing boxes are preset to sell 500 shares. One is set to route a limit order to Island, while the other is set to route to SOES. The SOES order is set at market. This may have to be changed to a limit order if conditions warrant. By setting up this selling configuration you are ready to hit an ECN *or* a market maker. All you have to do is click on the market maker screen to fill in the price on Island and hit the sell button or, alternatively, hit the sell button for SOES. It will send a market order.

Order-Routing Tactics Using Level II Information

One of the most important things to learn about Level II information is when and how to route the order using Island, SOES, Archipelago (TNTO, ARCHIP, ARCA) and Super DOT. You will see several examples of different Level II screens in the next few pages. Because the Level II screen changes very quickly, you need to understand which route is best for buying or selling at a given moment. Understanding the best route for your buy, sell, or short order will put you ahead of the game and give you confidence.

Buying Examples

The following example shows NITE, a market maker, in the active market at the bid and SHWD, also a market maker, at the ask:

Bid	Ask
$\frac{3}{16}$	
NITE $\frac{1}{8}$	SHWD $\frac{1}{4}$

If you wanted to attempt to buy on the bid, you could bid for stock along with NITE on Island. Island would appear just under NITE, both showing the same price, say 30⅛. By going alongside NITE in this case, the two of you are what is referred to as *national best bid or offer* (NBBO). You could also bid for stock at a higher price than NITE, say ³⁄₁₆. If you wanted to buy the stock at the ask, 30¼, you would route to a SOES market. The preceding example assumes that you are buying into the beginning of a rise in the stock price. Any time you have any of 500 market makers at the ask, you can route a SOES market order.

In the following case, you would use Island to buy on the bid and SOES to buy on the ask:

Bid	Ask
ISLD	GSCO
Island	SOES

Here you would use SOES to buy on both sides:

Bid	Ask
MASH	HEZG
SOES	SOES

In this example, you would use Island to buy on both sides:

Bid	Ask
ISLD	ISLD
Island	Island

In the following example, if price is moving up and it looks like you are going to break through resistance at $40⅜, you can bid for the stock at $40⁵⁄₁₆. Should you get filled at that price, you can get out at $40¼ if you are wrong.

If you want to short, expecting the stock to break through support, you can enter on a plus tick or a zero-plus tick just above support, $40⅛ or $40¹⁄₁₆. If you are wrong and a SOES market maker is on the bid, enter a SOES market order. If a stock is running with momentum and you want to enter, you hit whomever is at the bid or the ask to enter the trade.

In this next example, you would want to use ARCA to hit the offer (ask) because if INCA lifts its offer, ARCA will hit GSCO at ¾ (the same procedure would be used to cover a short position):

Bid	Ask
NITE ⅝	INCA 1¹⁄₁₆
	GSCO ¾
	ARCA

In the following example, if you wanted to buy back 1,000 shares you would use ARCA to hit REDI for 500 and BRUT for the other 500. This would fill your order at ¹¹⁄₁₆. This would be a better strategy than trying to hit GSCO with a SOES order at ¾. If GSCO is refreshing, it has 17 seconds to fill your order, and a lot can change in 17 seconds. Also remember the SOES five-minute rule. You have to wait five minutes before you can buy or sell another 1,000 shares using the SOES system.

Bid	Ask	
MASH ⅝	REDI ¹¹⁄₁₆	500
	BRUT ¹¹⁄₁₆	700
	GSCO ¾	1000
	ARCA	

The following example shows two different ways of handling a buy to cover. First, if you needed to buy only 1,000 shares, you would use ISLD. But if you needed the 2,000 shares offered by INCA, you would use ARCA to hit INCA, but remember, SelectNet preference gives INCA 20 seconds to acknowledge your order. Also remember that ARCA allows you to hit an ECN when an ECN is at the inside bid or offer (ask).

Bid	Ask	
ISLD ⅝	ISLD ¹¹⁄₁₆	1000
	GSCO ¹¹⁄₁₆	1000
	INCA ¹¹⁄₁₆	2000
	Island	ARCA

Selling Examples

Selling your stock at the bid (termed *hit the bid*) is simply a matter of perceiving whether a market maker or an ECN is at the bid.

When a stock is starting to move up on momentum, you may want to offer out your stock on the ask with a market maker using Island showing ⅜ or, alternatively, improve the market by becoming the lowest offer in the country at ⁵⁄₁₆ using ISLD. This would be done only if you wanted to sell the stock at once.

Bid		Ask		⅛
				⁵⁄₃₂
			⁵⁄₁₆	³⁄₁₆
NITE	⅛	SHWD	⅜	¼
		ISLD	⅜	⁹⁄₃₂
				⁵⁄₁₆
				¹¹⁄₃₂
SOES		Island		⅜

Here are two more examples of selling using SOES and Island. The route simply depends on whether a market maker or an ECN is at the bid or the ask.

Bid	Ask	Bid	Ask
ISLD	GSCO	ISLD	ISLD
Island	SOES	Island	Island

Intraday Trading Tactics

Figure 6.13 shows a Level II screen of Gillette, which is traded on the NYSE. At this point, the stock shows the potential of becoming a high-probability short. There is an uptick, so the short trade can be made. The stock is sold short at 12:11 P.M.

The strategy that led to this decision was based on technical factors. First, the five-minute chart shows that the stock had a parabolic run, putting in a rounded top just below 42½. At this point the stock looked like the momentum had run out. If Gillette fell to the 17-period EMA or below, the reward-to-risk ratio would be acceptable. The 15-minute chart also showed a very small high-low range bar, just under $42½. Gillette also had a strong support level at $41¾. The S&P 500 at this time looked weak and began to turn down sec-

---

Figure 6.13 Shorting Gillette
Used with permission of Townsend Analytics, Ltd.

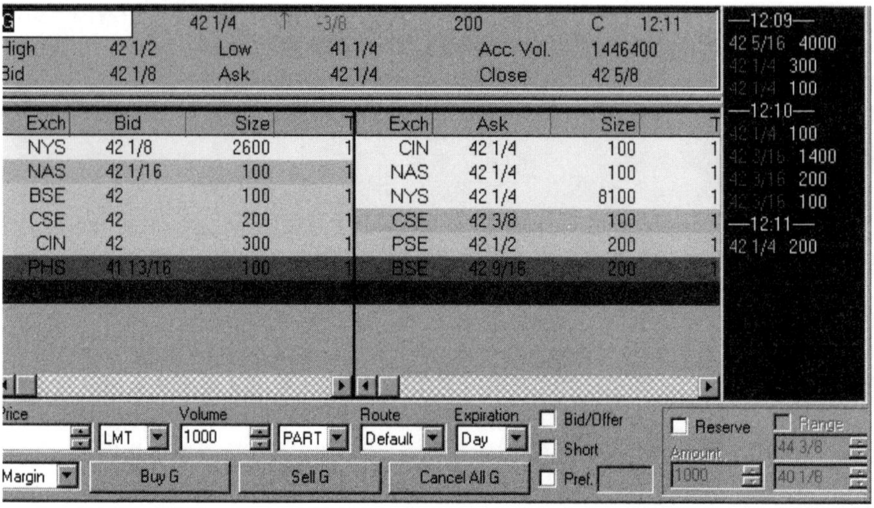

onds after the short position was taken. Figure 6.14 shows the Level II screen just after the short position was covered. The stock was bought back at $42¹³⁄₁₆, and seconds later, Gillette began to rally back to resistance at $42.

Figure 6.15 shows a five-minute chart of Gillette. You see the parabolic run beginning just prior to 11:30 A.M. The rounded top formation occurs between 11:35 and 11:45 A.M., followed by a penetration of the 7-period EMA and subsequently the 17-period EMA. Figure 6.16 shows a 15-minute bar chart of Gillette. Note the parabolic run and the high-low range bar at the top. This confirmed the possibility of a reversal.

The Double Play

Whenever you take a short position intraday, you must be aware of any support areas that may cause the stock to reverse its downward trend. If the support is far enough below your entry point and at or near even numbers, an opportunity may exist. I call this the *double play*. If you are short 500 shares and feel very confident that the stock will in fact reverse trend at that predetermined area, you

Figure 6.14 Buy to cover Gillette
Used with permission of Townsend Analytics, Ltd.

G		41 7/8	↓ -3/4		300		N	13:00	41 13/16	200
High	42 1/2	Low	41 1/4		Acc. Vol.	1698000			41 13/16	100
Bid	41 7/8	Ask	41 15/16		Close	42 5/8			—12:58—	

Exch	Bid	Size	T	Exch	Ask	Size	T
NYS	41 7/8	1000	1	NAS	41 15/16	100	1
NAS	41 13/16	100	1	NYS	41 15/16	1000	1
CSE	41 3/4	100	1	CIN	42 1/16	200	1
CIN	41 3/4	200	1	BSE	42 1/8	100	1
PSE	41 3/4	700	1	CSE	42 1/8	100	1
PHS	41 9/16	100	1	PSE	42 7/16	100	1
BSE							

Right column data:
41 7/8 2400
41 13/16 300
41 7/8 500
—12:59—
41 7/8 1000
41 15/16 4000
41 13/16 500
41 15/16 4000
41 15/16 2500
41 15/16 2500
41 15/16 100
—13:00—
41 15/16 100
41 7/8 300

Price: 41 13/16 LMT — Volume: 1000 — Route: PART — Default — Expiration: Day — ☐ Bid/Offer — ☐ Reserve — ☐ Range — Amount 44

Margin — Buy G — Sell G — Cancel All G — ☐ Short — ☐ Pref. NAS — 1000 — 39 13/16

Figure 6.15 Five-minute chart of Gillette
Used with permission of Townsend Analytics, Ltd.

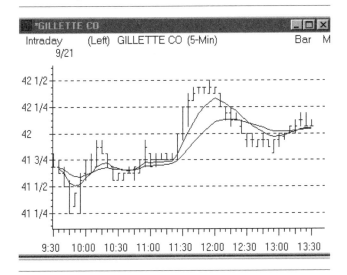

*GILLETTE CO

Intraday   (Left) GILLETTE CO (5-Min)   Bar   M
9/21

Figure 6.16 Fifteen-minute chart of Gillette
Used with permission of Townsend Analytics, Ltd.

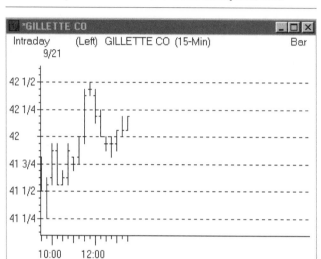

can place a buy limit order for 1,000 shares. Your 500 shares from the short position will be covered, locking in a profit, and you automatically go long 500 shares. The 500 shares you are long will ride the rebound in trend for as long as it lasts. If you are wrong and the stock continues to go lower, simply sell your long position. I use this technique on numerous occasions with excellent results. Check with your electronic broker to see if you may use this tactic. Company procedures dictate this policy. For example, the placement of stop orders on the Nasdaq is a company decision.

Figure 6.17 shows a five-minute bar chart of Home Depot after shorting the stock at $66¼. You are in an excellent downtrend that lasts until the stock hits $65½. As the stock begins to slow its downward momentum at $65⅝, you place a buy limit order for 1,000 shares at $65½. Price stabilizes at $65½ and begins to rise. You covered your short position of 500 shares, taking a profit, and automatically went long 500 at $65½. As the trend began to stabilize above the 7- and 17-period EMAs, the S&P 500 began to trend downward. The stock began to move slightly lower. You sell Home Depot at

Figure 6.17   Five-minute chart on Home Depot
Used with permission of Townsend Analytics, Ltd.

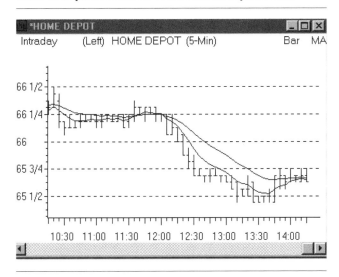

$65¹⁵⁄₁₆, taking your profit twice on one stock. You now look for another high-probability trade.

Fibonacci Retracement Lines

Fibonacci was a mathematician who was born in the thirteenth century in Italy. Modern traders pay homage to his work every day in the market when they use Fibonacci lines to anticipate price support or reversal. Before you take a long or short position, I strongly suggest as part of your screening process that you identify not only support and resistance but also the Fibonacci lines. Many times, price will rally from or break below Fibonacci lines. When the lines coincide with support or resistance areas, they tend to be important points from which price moves in one direction or another. Figure 6.18 shows Fibonacci lines on a daily chart. Remember where and at what price you encounter the Fibonacci lines. If you are trading intraday, do not forget at what price the Fibonacci lines occurred.

The Fibonacci retracement lines in Figure 6.18 are calculated from a line drawn from point 1 and ending at point 2. The calculation

Figure 6.18 Fibonacci retracement lines
Used with permission of Townsend Analytics, Ltd.

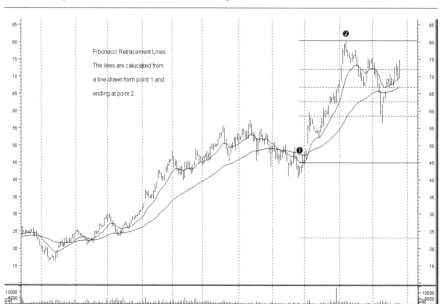

can be done by most technical analysis software. Remember, at or near Fibonacci lines, price will usually move in a defined direction.

In Chapters 1 through 6, you learned statistical and technical information about trading. Unfortunately, this will not be enough to make you a successful trader. All of the technology and technical skill in the world will be useless to you unless you can control emotional decisions. In Chapter 7, you are going to learn about the *next evolution in trading.* You will come to understand how you can be trained to reach a level of control and focus beyond what you think is possible. Chapter 7 is the key that will unlock your potential as a trader and open the door to previously unrealized performance. The challenge of Chapter 7 is to understand and accept that your potential lies not in technology but in biomechanical training.

chapter 7

the biomechanical trader

A *biomechanical trader* is one who is aware that trading is influenced by human physiology and who has achieved the highest level of mental and physical control. *Biomechanical training,* created and designed by Robert Deel, enhances the trader's performance by increasing emotional control, concentration, focus, and reaction time. The biomechanical trader has a distinct advantage over an individual who has not experienced the proper mental and physical conditioning. In this chapter, you'll learn about my powerful new concept for trading.

The Hunter

Primitive humans used their intelligence and creativity to become the dominant force on our planet. In competition for dominance of the species, human beings had to develop physically and mentally to the challenges of a hostile world. It is highly likely that primitive people's senses were more highly developed than those of modern humans. Survival for primitive people depended on these very senses. To successfully compete in this environment, humans developed tools for hunting and gathering food and for protection against other species who were physically superior. The human brain ultimately won the battle for survival by dominating over sharp teeth and claws in the primitive world. Over time, human creativity led to the development of mechanical machines that freed people from labor-intensive tasks. With the invention of machines and technology humans have come to dominate the modern world in much the same way that sharp tools helped them become masters of the prehistoric world.

Today, people have become totally dependent on mechanization and technology. Nowhere is it more evident than in the arena of trading the stock market. It is my firm belief that your success or failure trading the market will not be the mastery of technology, but the mastery of the biomechanical machine that is *you*. It will be the awakening of senses and reflexes of our primitive past that will lead you to your success in the market. Hunting and trading require the same skills: physical and mental stamina, focus, concentration, fast reflexes and reaction time, an elevation of the senses such as visual and auditory perception. For the modern trader, these abilities or biological skills have been dulled by the narcotic dependence on technology.

Today we are surrounded by the marvels of technology. We are the direct beneficiaries of a revolution in affordable computer software and hardware technologies. Unfortunately, many of us look to technology to provide the answers that we seek, and when technology fails us we are lost. Relying on technology for successful trading is doomed to failure. The answer isn't inside the box (computers or software): The answer to becoming a successful trader lies within *you,* the *biomechanical trader.* As a biomechanical being, you are far more complex than any computer yet devised. You make the buy and sell decisions; you and only you are responsible for your success.

If computers, trading systems, and magic formulas had the answers, then we would all be rich. Obviously, this is not the case. The trading system is only as good as the trader trading it. You could take 10 individuals, provide them all with $100,000, give them exactly the same trading system, computer, software, knowledge, even *commission-free* trading—and the majority would lose money. All 10 will have different results. Why? The answer to this question could very well be your financial wake-up call. The difference is the individual mind-set of each trader and an awareness that there is a mind-body connection to trading. That mental state of mind is called the *alpha zone*. Individuals who enter the alpha zone have an emotional control and focus that the others don't have. You could take traders who have the proper biomechanical awareness, give them a ruler, pencil, hand-held calculator, and chart book, and they will outperform those who rely on technology in the box. Traders do not lose money because of technology. Most of the time they lose because of emotionally driven decisions. Traders relying on technology usually live in denial and avoid the real problem. Whenever they lose money, they think the answer to the problem is simply to buy more technology. They are always looking for the answer in the box. It hasn't occurred to them that *they* might be the problem. Until you face the fact that your success lies in becoming the new biomechanical trader, success will elude you. The biomechanical trader uses technology while realizing that it is *only a tool* and nothing more. Success or failure is up to the individual trader making the trade.

Looking for the Edge

The whole focus of looking for a competitive edge in trading has always been in the area of technology. Anyone can buy the newest computer technology and software, so there is no real advantage that you can gain that someone else won't have the next day. The real edge will be gained not by the improvement of technology, but by the improvement of the men and women who are trading. We are all biomechanical devices, unique and complex, and as human machines we can improve. Everyone realizes that exercising our physical bodies will improve them. These changes are forged in the fire of our will, which is in fact a state of mind. If the mind controls the body, which is matter, why then can't the mind control the psychological environment that is the market? The market is not physical—it is mental. Each tick that appears in a real-time chart had its origin in the mind of a trader before the electronic pulse displayed his or her intentions to buy or sell. The psychological effects of fear and greed are states of mind and are not part of our physical reality. You can't touch fear, greed, or other emotions, yet they have an undeniable effect on you in your corporeal world.

By understanding the mind-body connection of trading you will achieve a tempo of performance you have never before experienced. This is the edge that every trader in the world is looking for. Once you seek out and learn the mental and physical disciplines of biomechanical trading, you will have an edge that others only dream of. The edge is *not* in the box. The edge lies in the improvement of your mental and physical control and mastery of your own emotions.

The Science of Biology and Trading

Understanding and learning about key biological factors that affect your trading performance is of the utmost importance. This information can give you an understanding and an awareness that few traders possess. With this information, it is possible to mentally and physically change, improving on the old model with measurable results. Let's examine several biological factors that affect us as traders and aggressive investors.

Genetics

The first step along the path to understanding ourselves must begin with a look at genetics. Your DNA is to a large degree responsible for your physical and mental abilities. Like it or not, you are born with a biological blueprint, and we all go through life learning to accept our genetic positives and negatives. In the year 2003, a biological revolution will unfold: The Human Genome Project will be completed, delivering an accurate DNA sequence representing the genetic blueprint of the human species. For the first time, humans will have the book of life.

Scientists will be able to treat diseases by isolating genes that cause human ailments; they will be able to correct genetic abnormalities. For the first time in recorded human history, it will be possible to change humankind on a genetic level. The ethical, moral, and religious implications of this are, of course, profound. Only the future will reveal how we use this power to change humankind.

From this monumental project comes interesting information. Your ability to accept levels of risk may in fact be genetic in nature. It has been assumed that risk taking was entirely psychological in nature. There seems to be evidence of a gene that researchers called the *risk gene.* The gene, known as D4DR, has been associated with individuals who are risk takers. Another recently discovered gene seems to regulate anxiety. If one has less of gene D4DR and more of the anxiety gene, that individual may be very risk averse. It may be that a balance of the two genes, combined with social and human experience, contributes to one's success or failure in the stock market. This information is based on recent data from the Human Genome Project.

Biological Time and Trading

Let me ask you a simple question. Are you a day person or night person? Are you an individual who wakes up in the morning ready to take on the world, or are you an individual who becomes more alert as the day goes on? Your answer to this question has some profound implications for you as a modern trader. Your biological clock was first set in the dawn of primitive time. Humans hunted during the day and slept during the night. Other species fed during the night and slept during the day, developing what we call *nocturnal cycles.* Homo sapiens developed a 24-hour biological time cycle. Within this cycle, biological and chemical events take place that affect your life and your trading performance.

Circadian Rhythms

Circadian (pronounced sir-KAY-dee-in) rhythms are controlled by a biological clock in the human brain. The *supachiasmatic nucleus* (SCN for short) is that clock. It is located within the hypothalamus of the brain. The SCN is strongly influenced by changes between sunlight and darkness and is sensitive to minute changes in light. It can tell the difference between morning sunlight, midday, and of course, night. Light information is transferred to the SCN by the retina, which interprets this information and passes it on to the pineal gland, which secretes the hormone melatonin. Melatonin regulates the 24-hour cycle. Darkness causes a rise in the secretion of hormone, while light inhibits it. Alertness and sleep are affected by the control of light. Is your trading area a dark dungeon? I don't know why traders seem to want to trade in the basement or in the darkest part of the office or house where they have no natural light. The lack of light will affect your alertness and your cognitive thinking. If you are a *night person,* starting off your trading day in a dark room with no natural light will affect your level of concentration, focus, and reaction time. If the room is warm and if there is a continuous sound such as a clock, computer hum, or flickering light, you may have found the reason why you just can't seem to do well in the opening hours of the market. First, if you are a night person, you aren't *biologically suited* for early-morning trading. If you have to trade in the morning, you are going to have to reset your biological clock. Yes, this can be done. Airline pilots must do this on international flights that cross time-date zones. My advice would be *not* to go against your biology. A biomechanical trader will do what is necessary to perform at optimum efficiency. If possible, start your trading day later and trade more at the end of the day when your mind is more alert. A morning person would simply do the reverse, trading the first part of the day to take advantage of an alert, focused mind. As you have learned in previous chapters, the first two hours and last two and one-half hours of the trading day exhibit the highest probability for success. Is it coincidence that this time frame just happens to fit human circadian cycles? I don't think so. I am convinced that a large part of the cycles in the market are, in fact, related to circadian biological cycles. If you think about it, the market is a human creation, and it is our trading that gives it life. It should, therefore, reflect the cycles of its creators.

If you are a professional trader and your job demands that you trade, you can't go to your boss and say, "My individual circadian rhythms won't enable me to be at my best until later in the day so I am going to wait before I start trading." Your boss is going to think you have lost your mind. If you find yourself in a situation in which you can't adjust your trading hours, I have some very helpful suggestions to assist you in keeping alert throughout the trading day.

Muscular Activity   Most traders sit in a comfortable chair, while some stand at their trading stations; both lead to fatigue. Stretching can alleviate fatigue by triggering the sympathetic nervous system, which helps keep you alert. Another simple exercise is to squeeze a small rubber ball or wrist exerciser, which will also stimulate muscular activity. A walk or run in the early morning, preferably in morning light, will stimulate your body alertness.

Food and Nutritional Supplements   Do *not* start the day by consuming sugar. If you do, in most cases you are setting yourself up for a drop in alertness later in the afternoon. When trading through the lunch hour, many traders now eat energy bars. If you do this, make sure that these bars don't have a large percentage of sugar. If they do, it will exacerbate a period of decreased alertness that some people call the "lunch dip" or "afternoon dip," which occurs between the hours of 1:00 P.M. and 4:00 P.M. Within these hours, performance suffers, and if you are in one of those dimly lit trading dungeons, you have to fight to stay awake. If you are on the East Coast of the United States, you are trading during this time frame. This dip in alertness has nothing to do with lunch; rather, it is related to human circadian rhythms. Fluctuations in body temperature, hormone levels, and other activities in the human brain cause a perceptible drop in alertness during that time. We experience peak alertness in the morning and early evening. The Mexican culture has what is called *siesta* (midday nap), and life and business revolve around this practice. Mexicans simply extend their day into the early evening hours. In the United States, we see this as a waste of time, but from a biological point of view they are operating at a time when they are the most alert. Some major corporations in the United States are now adopting the idea of short naps to increase the productivity and alertness of their corporate executives and employees. The companies that have adopted this program see the results in less absenteeism, increased productivity, and greater company loyalty. Even Japanese corporations recognize the importance of naps to increase productivity. Human biology is essentially the same no matter what part of the world you live in.

The type of food you eat and the time you eat it are important from a biological point of view. I love a good turkey sandwich. If I were trading on the East Coast and had turkey for lunch, I would be compounding the problem of decreased alertness—the afternoon dip previously described. Turkey has within it a substance called *tryptophan,* which will cause relaxation and drowsiness. If I eat a turkey sandwich just prior to 1:00 P.M. the combination of normal human circadian rhythm and the chemical effect of the tryptophan can cause a marked drop in performance. Other foods that have tryptophan include fish and egg whites. Foods like bananas or milk help induce sleep. Foods or drinks with caffeine (chocolate, tea, soft drinks, herbs like green tea, gurana, and gotakola) stimulate the body and help to inhibit sleep. Don't get into a habit of using caffeine to stimulate awareness.

Temperature   Dry, cool air will help keep an individual alert. Conversely, a warm or humid temperature will make you sleepy. Your age and sex will also impact how temperature affects you. As we get older, physiological changes take place and we tend to be less tolerant of colder temperatures. An increase in external temperature tends to make an individual drowsy. Studies have shown that men and women perceive and regulate body temperature differently. Women tend to become much colder than men in the same temperature environment. This explains the battle over temperature control between men and women that has been raging for years. It has a biological basis.

Light   You should increase the brightness of the light in your trading environment. If possible, have as much natural light as you can. Bright light will stimulate alertness. In some cases, you can increase the light in your trading area by using a desk or floor lamp. Your light source should approximate natural light. Be careful not to increase the temperature in your trading area, as this will cause you to become drowsy. Remember that darkness increases the production of melatonin, which brings on fatigue and sleep.

Sound   Sound can either stimulate or bring on relaxation and sleep depending on the type of sound. Listen to the sounds in your trading area and be on guard for sounds that will cause you to become drowsy. These sounds would have a dull, repetitive nature, such as the sounds of technology that surround a trading environment—for example, computer hum or buzz, overhead-light hum, or any continuous monotone sound. Sounds that stimulate would be irregular or variable in nature, such as TV, radio, or loud talking. These sounds can become distracting, and you need to focus on what you are doing. When talking or some other irregular sound becomes distracting, I suggest that you use soft earplugs. In fact, the use of earplugs has been shown to enable readers to concentrate and focus more effectively on written material.

Sight   Don't sit and stare at your computer monitors. Becoming fixed on one spot of the screen will send you into a daydream state. Move your eyes and head slightly to the right and left and remain focused on trading. Make sure your computer monitors have a dot pitch of 0.25 or 0.26 mm, or your eyes will become irritated and fatigued.

Smell   Our olfactory sense, or sense of smell, is one of the most powerful senses we have. It has both a conscious and subconscious effect on our mind and body. You can confirm this by popping an ammonia capsule under the nose of an unconscious person: The sense of smell will return the individual to a conscious state. Aroma can stimulate or induce relaxation. The smell of peppermint can induce alertness, while the smell of jasmine or lavender can relax and calm you. In my office I have a time-release spray (see Figure 7.1) that is set to spray the scent of peppermint at 11:00 A.M. and again at 12:00 P.M. Pacific time. I have found that it increases my alertness and helps fight off normal circadian fatigue. I know that the last two and one-half hours of the trading day have a high prob-

Figure 7.1   Time-release atomizer

ability for success, and I want to take advantage of this potential opportunity by being as alert as possible. Such an atomizer can be placed on your desk or in your office and set to release at specific times of the day.

Reversing Circadian Rhythms

One of the most important factors influencing circadian rhythms is the degree of light and darkness your body experiences. Everyone is no doubt familiar with the effects of *jet lag,* which is a disruption of the circadian cycle brought on by crossing time zones faster than the body can adjust. Airline pilots have to deal with this problem all the time. You can adjust your circadian rhythms (biological clock) by exposing your eyes to bright light at specific times during the day. It is quite possible to adjust your biological clock to a new time zone within one day. In fact, natural adaptation could take a month. To speed up the process, you can use specific artificial light to accomplish the adjustment. If you are a professional trader, or if it's

Miami today and London or Tokyo tomorrow, adjusting your circadian rhythm will give you a definite advantage.

Sleep

It is important that a trader learns about sleep. Not just because sleep is necessary for performance and alertness, but because in sleep you naturally enter four different states of mind. The concept of entering a different state of mind to improve your trading seems ridiculous to most traders. What they don't understand is that all human beings enter different states of mind every night. Two of these states of mind, which you have entered all of your life while sleeping, hold the key to your trading performance. There is nothing ridiculous about improving your trading. It is ridiculous to let ignorance and a misplaced trust in technology cause you to fail.

Nuclear accidents, plant explosions, fatal fires, and other tragic events may be linked to fatigue and a disruption of the circadian cycle. Studies suggest that 50 percent of fatal highway accidents are caused by fatigued drivers. The estimated cost of worldwide losses due to fatigue is more than $370 billion. The inability to sleep seems to increase as we get older. The body's ability to regulate temperature and melatonin production decrease with age. As we get older, we tend to have fewer SCN neurons. Trying to trade when you are fatigued or don't feel well is not in your best interests and could cause you to become a market statistic.

The type and amount of sleep you get is very important. Sleep is not like some people imagine it. You don't just shut down and wake up after a set number of hours. Sleep has several stages, each distinguished by different brain-wave activities that recur throughout the night. I suspect that everyone has had the feeling of freefalling in a dream. It is interesting to note that we fall and then rise through the different levels of sleep. There are four stages of sleep, which include both non-REM (rapid eye movement) sleep and REM sleep. You can record the different levels of sleep by the use of an electroencephalogram (EEG) machine because each level of sleep has a different frequency. This makes it possible to identify the state of mind we want to access as traders. Let's examine the different levels of sleep.

Levels of Sleep In your conscious state, when you are awake and feel alert, your brain-wave pattern is known as *beta*. When you lie down to sleep and begin to feel drowsy, your brain begins to produce *alpha* waves. It is important to understand that each state of consciousness has a different brain-wave pattern and frequency. This enables a trained professional to identify different states of consciousness. Alpha and theta waves will be explored later when we discuss how we use hypnosis and biofeedback in training the biomechanical trader. For now, you need to understand the basic mechanics of the sleep process.

> *Level 1:* After about five to seven minutes of alpha-wave production, you reach the twilight of consciousness. Now the brain changes wave production to the *theta* wave. In level 1, you have definite relaxation of breathing and muscles and slower pulse rate. In other words, a state of mind influences matter, and the matter in this case is you. Never let anyone tell you that a state of mind has no effect on you or your performance.

> *Level 2:* This stage usually lasts for 15 to 35 minutes and is characterized by flashes of electric activity within the brain.

> *Level 3:* Levels 3 and 4 are our deepest levels of sleep, during which the brain is producing *delta* waves. Deep sleep will usually last for 30 to 40 minutes.

> *Level 4:* This is the last stage of descent into sleep. From level 4, the sleeper begins to ascend upward, passing levels 3 and 2 until reaching level 1 and beginning REM sleep. REM sleep represents about 25 percent of total sleep time. If you awaken during REM sleep, you are able to remember dreams. Learning, creativity, imagination, and suggestion response come in REM sleep. The *alpha brain wave* is predominant in this state of mind. When you meditate, you enter level 1 and begin to relax: You have willed yourself into a different state of mind. A typical REM cycle can last for minutes or up to an hour. During the night, you will

pass through cycles of REM and non-REM sleep, with each cycle lasting around 90 minutes.

The Sleeper Awakens   How many times have you awakened from sleep feeling disoriented and unable to think straight? In fact, you may find it hard to talk because you just can't formulate what you want to say. The level of sleep you are in determines how alert you will be when you awaken. If you awake from delta, or deep sleep, you will feel many of the feelings I have just described. This condition may last for more than 5 to 10 minutes. However, if you awaken from levels 1 or 2, you feel alert and even refreshed. A biomechanical trader uses this information to help his or her performance in trading the market. It is possible to control or manage your sleep cycle. You can learn techniques that will enable you to wake up from the correct level of sleep for better performance. Understanding that levels 1 and 2 will refresh you can be an important factor in mental performance. If you did not get enough rest, it is possible to learn to relax and place yourself in an alpha or theta state. Within this state of mind, you can refresh your mind and relax your body, in effect giving yourself a mental and biological recharge. You can use this technique during the time of day when alertness suffers—from 1:00 to 4:00 P.M. This will help you combat the natural circadian cycle known as "afternoon dip," or "lunch dip."

About now you should feel warm and sleepy. You may feel drowsy. Your eyes may feel heavy. You might even be yawning. Reading about the states of sleep has made you tired. If this is the case, you have been influenced on a subconscious level to become sleepy. The process started from the title "Sleep." The wording, sentence structure, and the subject have been set up to induce a relaxed, calm state and induce an alpha response. Have a good night's sleep and a profitable day trading tomorrow!

We will examine other biological factors later in this chapter when we discuss factors involved in the mechanics of creating a biological trader. Let's now examine psychological factors and characteristics that you need to become aware of before we take a further look into the creation of a biomechanical trader.

Psychological Factors and Personality

Emotions play an extremely important role in trading, but many traders ignore them or minimize their importance. Ignoring emotions does not make them go away. It just weakens your control over their effects on your trading. In Chapter 1 you learned that you must adopt a trading strategy that fits your individual personality. If you do not, the chances of failure are very high. One characteristic of successful traders is an early identification of strengths and weakness. Successful traders maximize their strengths and try to minimize their weaknesses, but to do this you must first know and understand yourself. What kind of trading personality are you? I'm going to profile three broad types of trading personalities that fit most people. Chances are, one of the three will fit your personality. If you see traits in yourself that are not complimentary, don't become defensive and deny them. Becoming a biomechanical trader means seeing what is true and accepting both the positive and the negative. Once you see yourself honestly, you can begin the transformation psychologically. This is the first step in developing a trader's state of mind, whereby you control the market instead of the market controlling you.

Three Trading Personalities

Dominant Trader Dominant personalities want to be in control. They analyze everything, looking for signs of weakness they can exploit. They are intensely competitive and must win at all costs. Business, golf, even parties are a contest. They need to make lots of money, have the best golf score, and be the center of attention at parties. They think of life as a vertical arrangement with themselves being at or near the top of the order. Most dominant personalities are status conscious. They are ambitious, tough, aggressive, manipulative, somewhat closed minded and insensitive. To them life is a contest that has winners and losers, and they can't afford to think about abstract subjects like other people's feelings. This would distract them from the only thing that matters to them: *winning.* Dominant traders deny their own tender emotions, and denying these emotions prevents them from controlling their effects. They refuse to admit they have weaknesses, need affection, and have certain dependency needs. They dislike these aspects of their personality so much that they overreact and behave tougher than they really are. Because winning is so important, extremely dominant people will do whatever it takes to win. Because they will do anything to win, they assume others will do the same. As a result, they distrust others.

Dominant personalities are independent and individualistic. Taking orders, accepting advice, or following the rules are seen as weaknesses. They insist on doing things their way and will break the rules to do so. They are afraid of losing, of showing weakness, and of admitting their fears. They overreact and become excessively dominant. A dominant personality will display nonverbal signs of communication, such as clenched fists and jabbing motions with a finger, pencil, or pen. A dominant personality tends to be very short tempered, raising his or her voice and becoming red-faced and angry. The anger and nonverbal communication are used in an attempt to dominate you. These people want and need to be in control, and the one thing over which they have no control is the market. This frustrates and confounds them. They yell and scream, yet the market pays no attention to their raving. The market ignores their roar, which frustrates them further.

Dominant personalities are impatient; they want you to get to the point right away. They feel they know what you need and don't have any qualms about telling you so. They tend to dominate conversation by talking faster and louder than the person with whom they are talking. Dominant traders never admit to being wrong without blaming some external circumstance. They don't accept the fact that *they* may have made a mistake or error, because doing so would be admitting to weakness, and a dominant personality would rather submit to a root canal than to say, "I was wrong."

Dominant traders are quick to become frustrated when their routines are disturbed or when changes occur that they have not agreed to. They like a controlled environment in which they set the rules. This is why they react so strongly to the market. Dominant personalities are poor listeners. They frequently interrupt conversations and don't like being asked the same question over again. "I just told you," or, "Weren't you listening?" are their responses. They tend to be insensitive on the surface and uncomfortable with emotional subjects. Even though they are repelled by emotion in others, they can't see their own emotional reactions. This is because they don't want to face their real fear: an acknowledgment of emotions, which they see as a flaw in their personality. To become a biomechanical trader, all of us have to face our fears and understand ourselves.

Detached Trader   A detached personality tends to put off dealing with a problem, hoping that if he or she ignores the problem it will go away. These types don't like confrontation and will avoid it rather than face it. Detached personalities have a fear of intimacy, dependency, and the uncertain and unpredictable. They tend to want to live in their own world, a world of rational thinking. They are more comfortable with machines, ideas, or numbers than with people. Drawn to order and predictability, their homes and checkbooks are in perfect order. Their desks or work areas may appear to be in disarray to an outsider, but it is organized confusion. The detached personality knows where everything is. Don't change anything on their desks because if you do they become severely upset. Minor deviations from their customary routines upset them. They suppress their own emotions and ignore other people's. They tend to be shy and aloof, putting up mental barriers to others and to their own success. They tend not to want to get too close or personally involved, fearing rejection.

Detached personalities are independent, yet readily accept authority, rules, and procedures, though they avoid people who attempt to control them. They are open-minded about impersonal issues and pride themselves on their objectivity. When confronted on a issue or opinion, they do not usually respond angrily. They look at the facts objectively and will change positions if the facts require it. They are thorough and are good listeners. They understand the unspoken personal boundaries of others.

The detached personality can't get enough facts. They overemphasize analysis and have to understand every single detail before they buy or sell. They think in logic and numbers and deal in facts. Detached trader personalities are good at solving problems that deal with logic. The detached trader is a rational thinker and thus goal oriented. He or she uses facts and logic to decide on an appropriate course of action to reach the goal. Unfortunately, the market isn't always logical. This confounds the detached personality because when something doesn't work, he or she tries to make it work based on logic and rational thinking. A detached personality may design a complex trading system but find it hard to trade that system because of his or her inner battle with risk and the fear of losing.

Detached personalities live by facts, logic, and laws (natural and human). They tend to seek order and are repulsed by the absence of it. Sometimes you can't find answers with logic and numbers. You may have to accept something on faith. This is almost more than a detached personality can stand because in their world everything is quantifiable.

Dependent Traders   The dependent personality is very social, wants to be liked, and needs the acceptance, understanding, and approval of others. These types are warm, friendly, and interested in people. They tend to be good listeners and are sensitive to other people's needs. Cooperative and compliant, they go along with other people's ideas because they don't want to elicit confrontation or anger. They are givers who want to help people, especially those who reward them with gratitude and affection.

Dependent personalities are very popular. However, they can be extremely insecure and needy of reassurance. Their demands can become so exhausting that people withdraw from them. This increases their insecurity. Dependent personalities are afraid of being alone, of rejection, and of conflict. Jealousy can be a serious problem for dependent personalities.

Dependent personalities will defy authority if they consider the authority to be unfeeling and unjust. They think and act impulsively. They are far more likely to place a trade out of impulse than out of any analysis. They have a feeling of integrity and they understand people. In fact, dependent personalities tend to be very empathetic of the problems of others. The words *feeling* and *understanding* are very much a part of who they see themselves to be.

Dependent personalities have an even greater fear of rejection than the detached trader, which makes them extremely risk conscious. You would think that given this fear of risk the dependent trader would be conservative, but this is not the case. Dependent traders are drawn to the market because they are attracted to danger. They are likely to have compulsive behaviors. They gather lots of information but don't assimilate it well. In most cases, the dependent personalities have problems with numbers and read slowly. Their comprehension and focus is poor because they are easily distracted. To compensate, dependent personalities are on an endless search for the best trading system or the next new software. Ironically, they tend to rely on personal verbal information and are usually looking for hot tips. Dependent personalities would rather talk about trading at a party than trade. They are attracted by social interaction and the rush they feel when they trade.

Use this information to better understand yourself. You can improve only by facing and accepting the truth about your nature. Biomechanical traders use this information to improve on their strengths and minimize their weaknesses. Recognizing your shortcomings is the first step to making them strengths.

Negative Psychological Characteristics of Traders

Now let's take a look at some of the factors that could negatively impact your trading. Forewarned is forearmed!

Foolishly Cheap   Do you really think it is smart to put $25,000 into an investment or trade without knowing what you are doing? Of course not, but you would be amazed at the number of people who won't spend $2,000 or $3,000 on an education because they think it is too much. These same people end up losing $20,000 that could have been avoided simply by spending $2,000, which doesn't seem very intelligent to me. Oddly, intelligence doesn't have anything to do with it. This is a psychological characteristic that many people have—and one that can cost you everything. Never think you are saving money by being foolishly cheap. You need tools, education, and software to be a success in the business of trading. Success doesn't usually go to the lowest bidder. If someone offers to sell you a diamond ring for a dime and you buy it, chances are that you just bought a diamond ring that isn't worth a dime.

Using this same philosophy to buy stock is doomed to failure. Buying or selling stock should have nothing to do with price. You buy or sell based on facts, both fundamental and technical. If you are undercapitalized you should *not* be trading. Individuals who are undercapitalized seek out cheap stocks. Stocks that are under $15 may have liquidity problems. Remember, cheap stocks can go to zero. Quality, on the other hand, may go down but it rarely goes to zero.

Never let price be a factor in your buying and selling decisions. If you are planning to trade electronically, you are going to need a minimum of $50,000 to $100,000. Electronic trading is no place for the foolishly cheap.

Instant Gratification Our society has become programmed for instant gratification. An impatience has seized our culture. We are no longer willing to wait—we want it and we want it now! Whole technologies have grown up around our insatiable appetite for faster results. We see it everywhere: one-hour photos, one-hour dry cleaning, and fast food. All around us are advertisements for the fastest modem or the fastest data delivery service. Any way you look at it, America is in a hurry. So let's all jump in our fast cars, buckle our safety belts, and get in the fast lane, because we all want to make money *fast,* don't we? This is one of the most destructive personality flaws an individual can have. The only thing you are going to get in a hurry is in trouble and broke. Electronic trading is a magnet that attracts individuals who are looking for answers in the box and want to make money *fast.* "Yep, step right up ladies and gentleman. Today—and today *only*—I have the answer for you in this attractive yet versatile box. It can buy on the bid and sell on the ask, and it can make money *fast.* Be the first in your neighborhood to lose money at the speed of light. You have done it the slow way—now do it the new improved fast way. Ladies and gentleman, with just a few clicks of the mouse you can leave behind the days of secure, boring financial independence and experience the thrill you get when you roll the dice in Las Vegas—all from the comfort of your own home or office."

Over many years of training traders and aggressive investors, I have learned the one sure path to losing money is trying to trade before you are ready. You need to know how to thoroughly analyze a stock and the market before you jump into something as potentially dangerous as trading electronically. You need to know how to trade long before you start using this technology, and most people do not. If you don't know what you are doing, the only thing electronic trading gives you is the potential to lose money exponentially. You must crawl before you walk and walk before you run. It is just common sense that you need knowledge and experience to succeed at anything.

I have witnessed firsthand people off the street trying to use electronic trading technology without even knowing what a moving average was or the most basic concepts of trend analysis. They did seem to be having fun losing money—which is what 92 percent of them will be doing, because they were shown only one method of trading: *scalping.* Scalping is great for the electronic trading firm but potentially dangerous for you. Typically, if you go back to that same firm in three months, you will see all new faces. Losing money wasn't so much fun after all. Slow down, get an impartial education, and stop trying to cut to the front of the line. That line is the losers' line, and there will always be space at the front.

Let's Get Rich Quick   Just for fun, I recently attended one of those get-rich-quick seminars. You know, the ones you hear about on radio or TV that always include the phrase, "I made more money than I did at my job." I now know that P. T. Barnum was right when he said, "There is a sucker born every minute." It seems that in America today people are grasping at anything that has any possibility of making money, no matter how outlandish it sounds. Do not mistake *marketing* for knowledge of the market. A rising stock market has drawn people who held CDs just a few years ago and who *never* before invested in stock. Now, these same people are trying to make money *trading,* an endeavor that they are not psychologically prepared for or trained to do. In their minds, the stock market always seems to go up. The thought of losing money never enters their heads. Well, trading is *not* for the novice or inexperienced. As I sat in this get-rich-quick stock seminar and looked around the room, all I could think of was fresh food. No, I wasn't hungry, but the market is a food chain in which the big, experienced fish devour the fish of little experience. What I saw was a true feeding frenzy in the making. Don't fall for get-rich-quick schemes, because if you do, you could make some well-trained professional trading shark very happy. The sweetest words a shark will ever hear are the words, "Let's all get rich quick." It's like ringing the dinner bell.

People trying to get rich quick are usually gamblers, and characteristically base their decisions on greed or financial desperation. These emotions will distort your judgment and create huge losses that will compound themselves. Your best chance of survival will be in learning to trade like a professional trader. Professionals don't try to break the bank and get rich quick. Professional traders know that the shark who survives the day will be around to trade tomorrow. If you try to get rich quick, you will only end up broke.

Ego Wall Street is paved with the bones of the traders who thought they were smarter than the market. People with huge egos have little chance of trading success. These people are usually the ones who are pontificating about their analysis of the market and are quick to anger when someone disagrees with them. They are always right. Don't worry, you won't have to endure them very long, because their big egos are going to attract big losses. The market loves to take the money of individuals with big egos because their money is the easiest to take. Being smarter than the market, they do some things that are sometimes hard to believe. Many times, you have to look twice at your screen because you just can't believe what you are seeing. After all, who are you to argue with genius? Just click that mouse and say, "Thank you very much."

Ego distorts rational thinking and causes people to take trades and positions that are against trend, momentum, and logic. The dominant personality is more likely to have a huge ego than is the detached or dependent personality type. Don't mistake confidence and experience with ego traders. Ego traders are trading out of emotional reactions or a knee-jerk response to an event. Ego traders usually lack the skill of fluid traders, who adapt to changes in market trend. Ego traders marry into a plan that is as fluid as cement and stay with it even when the trend has changed. Why don't they change? Because if they do they will have to admit to being wrong, and they would rather lose money than admit *they* could be wrong.

Education You go to school, gain an education, become employed, or start your own business. You learn basic month-to-month money management necessary to perform outside the arena of the stock market. You have been trained from childhood to think and to analyze problems, and this training and reflexive thinking cause many traders to fail. Success in trading or aggressive investing requires far more than formal education, computers, and software. Nothing in your education or work experience will prepare you for the psychological stresses that you will experience as aggressive investor or trader. Ninety percent of your success depends on the proper development of a trader's state of mind known as the *alpha zone*. You are going to learn about a revolutionary new training and mental conditioning system that will change the way you think about trading. Increased awareness and understanding will help you begin to prepare yourself to achieve the mental state necessary to enter the alpha zone, the realm of the biomechanical trader. The impact of this information will change your concept of trading from this day forward. From now on, you will view trading from a physiological and mental perspective. Let us examine the first step in becoming a biomechanical trader.

Creating the Biomechanical Trader

What makes supertraders consistently successful? It isn't that they are smarter than you are; it isn't that they have more money than you have; and it isn't that they have more knowledge than you have. Knowledge in and of itself will not make money for you in the market. While knowledge is power, knowledge without the ability to act on it and without emotional control is worthless. All the analysis and knowledge in the world will not do you any good unless you can pull the trigger when it comes time to buy or sell. Some of the most intelligent and knowledgeable people cannot trade successfully. For example, trading system designers who design systems for institutional traders and the public have a vast knowledge of trading and the mechanics of the markets, but most of them cannot trade effectively using their own trading systems. They lack mental focus and emotional control.

Successful traders perceive the internal and external world much differently than you do. They see more than is on the surface and tend to see connections between things very quickly. They tend to be very much in control of their emotions and have intense focus. When they trade, they are totally focused, yet fluid and able to quickly adapt to market volatility. They view losses not as a personal affront but as nothing more than the cost of doing business. They do not equate losses with personal failure. You win some, you lose some.

After doing the appropriate analysis they make decisions and act on them quickly. In almost every case, successful traders excel in the art of technical analysis. They see relationships in chart patterns and trends that others miss. This is because consistently successful traders tend to be visual and have the ability to see graphic relationships and patterns within price data.

The primary reason for the success of these traders is their ability to enter a totally different state of mind known as the *alpha zone*. It is difficult for most traders and aggressive investors to understand that success or failure is due to a state of mind. Athletes understand this concept very well. Today's modern athlete prepares mentally as well as physically for the game. All serious athletes credit this mental preparation for giving them an edge over their competition. Most battles are won or lost before the first shot is fired, and this preparation begins in the alpha zone.

The Alpha Zone

You have already learned that alpha is one of the four states of mind that we pass through on the way to and from sleep. Once you enter the alpha state, you are in a deep, relaxed state of alertness. Most people have the mistaken impression that when you are in an altered state of consciousness you are in a sleeplike state and not aware of what is going on around you. This is not the case when you are in the alpha zone. The biomechanical trader is trained to be able to enter the alpha zone at will. Why is this state of consciousness so important to a trader's success?

How would you like to have almost total concentration and focus? The ability to remember facts and details on demand? To be able to reprogram subconscious factors that are sabotaging you? How would you like to be able to relax for 10 minutes and feel like you had eight hours of sleep? How would you like to have control over your heartbeat, blood flow, and skin temperature? No, this isn't science fiction. It is scientifically possible. When you enter the alpha zone you have control over physical and psychological factors that few traders even know exists. Within four to six months, you can be trained to enter the alpha state. After your biomechanical training is complete, you can enter the alpha state at will.

When you enter the alpha state you are opening a door from the conscious to the subconscious mind. The subconscious mind can be influenced by *suggestion*. If you are convinced you can do something, you *believe* you can. Belief is one of the most powerful factors in our lives. Subconscious beliefs determine to a great extent whether we succeed or fail. Self-confidence is a belief in yourself, and it is one of the keys to your success. While you are in alpha state you are highly susceptible to suggestion, and thus an operator can begin to reprogram your subconscious mind. This is highly desirable because many psychological factors contributing to a trader's failure are found in the subconscious. To be successful, you have to truly believe you can operate on a subconscious level. When you enter alpha, your brain-wave pattern is from 8 to 13 cycles per second. This becomes the dominant brain-wave pattern, blocking the logical left-brain activity that filters out the subconscious. Once this mental guard is out of commission, you can access your creative mind, recall facts and information, focus, and achieve emotional control on a level you have not experienced before. Police departments and the FBI use hypnosis to put subjects into an alpha state whereby they can describe a crime scene in precise detail. Hypnosis allows the subject to view or relive a traumatizing experience without the emotional trauma or feeling.

Physical Control in Alpha   When individuals are in an alpha state they have control over their biological activity. In what is quite literally mind over matter, you can perform some amazing things. It is possible for a trained biomechanical trader to increase the temperature of his or her right or left hand at will or to slow heart rate and control blood pressure. It is even possible for a trained biomechanical trader to control blood flow. For example, if you were to take a pin and prick both index fingers, you could increase blood flow or stop it at will in either the right or left hand.

Scientists now believe that long-term memory is processed during sleep when you are in an alpha state. This information is effectively stored into long-term memory. This accounts for the ability of biomechanical traders to access memory and facts in great detail. You learn faster and remember more when you are in an alpha state, for you have the ability to focus the mind on one specific thing. In your conscious state, known as *beta,* you are continually processing external and internal information. In alpha state, inspiration comes to us in flashes of creativity. A perfect example of this is when you have been working on a problem all day and you just can't find the answer. You go to bed, and as you drift into sleep, the answer comes to you in a flash of inspiration. Research shows that the consolidation of information you already understand and have learned is accessed in the alpha state. If you think about the implications of training, the potential of both beta and alpha are truly amazing.

Another physical advantage that biomechanical training and the alpha zone gives you is *faster reaction time.* It is possible to increase the reaction time of a trader by 5 to 15 seconds. Younger and older traders alike can improve their reaction times.

What has all of this to do with trading? *Everything.* Imagine a trader with electronic trading technology who also has the physical and psychological control that biomechanical training provides. With their improved focus, emotional control, and faster reaction time, do you really think you can beat such traders? An intelligent person would join them, because you can't beat them. They are on the cutting edge in trading evolution. This is the edge every trader is looking for, and it cannot be found in the box.

Theta: The Other State of Mind

Theta is a state of deep relaxation. When you are in theta, your brain wave operates at 4 to 7 cycles per second. This is a deep state of awareness associated with dream control and the processing of daily information. Have you ever had strange dreams and, on analyzing them, realized that they were jumbled pieces of events you experienced over a short period of time? The brain is sorting out information that is being placed into long-term and short memory. Your visual brain sees only parts of this informational sorting process. This explains the jumbled images from your dreams.

The dreamscape, which is the theta state, can be reached only after long periods of meditation. Yogis who enter this state of mind can slow the heart to such an extent that, upon first examination, the pulse appears to be absent; breathing is so slow that the chest scarcely rises. In many cases the subject is so still that he or she appears to be dead. From this deep state of relaxation and consciousness you can achieve amazing mental and physical control. The theta state is the biomechanical trader's ultimate goal. When reached, the subconscious mind can be influenced even further. Once this is accomplished, the interference of negative subconscious programming can be eliminated. For the first time, you will be able to function on a mental level previously unknown to you. This is because most individuals use only the beta, or conscious, part of their mental ability. Beta represents only 12 percent of your mental capacity. After you experience biomechanical training, you will understand how to use the subconscious mind. The subconscious mind makes up the other 88 percent of mental capacity. You know the subconscious mind can be reached and reprogrammed through the alpha state and deep theta meditation. You are also now aware that memory and control of your body is possible in the alpha and theta states of consciousness. This is why state of mind is responsible for a trader's success or failure.

Hypnosis

Hypnosis is a tool accepted by the scientific community and used by thousands of individuals worldwide. Trying to deny that hypnosis exists or that it is not effective is a little like denying the world is round. Tradingschool.com uses hypnosis as part of a wide range of behavior-modification tools. To successfully create the biomechanical trader, many different tools are used, but hypnosis and biofeedback are first.

Hypnosis is used to help traders access the alpha state. From the alpha state, it is possible to influence the subconscious mind. You will do what the subconscious mind believes to be true. Because the subconscious believes what it is told, it is possible to circumvent the conscious mind and reprogram the subconscious mind with information that is positive for the trader. In the beginning of biomechanical training, you have two people working together: the student and the operator. The operator's presence is necessary to accomplish the initial reprogramming and to monitor the student's alpha state. At tradingschool.com, the pairing of student and operator is known as a *contact team.* The contact team works together for several months until the student shows that he or she can enter the alpha state through self-hypnosis. In reality, all hypnosis is self-hypnosis, because the student is the one who induces his or her own level of conscious relaxation. To make a change on the conscious level, you must first change the subconscious. The contact team can accomplish this over a short span of time.

Biofeedback

It is a scientific fact that your thoughts and emotions influence your body. You exhibit a physiological response to these thoughts and emotions, and this can be measured by the use of biofeedback equipment. For example, we know that the four different states of mind have different brain frequencies. Using biofeedback equipment, it is possible to monitor each state. During hypnosis, this equipment allows you to determine when the student is in an alpha state.

Reprogramming begins only when you can verify an alpha frequency of 7 to 13 cycles per second. Using biofeedback, the biomechanical trader can learn to control physiological and emotional responses much faster than with hypnosis alone. Reprogramming that may have taken years can be accomplished in a much shorter period of time. Tradingschool.com has been successful in creating biomechanical traders in a very short time frame. Four to six months is the normal training period for reprogramming traders, but in some cases, it takes a year. Reprogramming a lifetime of bad trading habits can't be accomplished overnight. Winners will take the time to improve and do whatever it takes. Losers never take the time to become successful. They are always in a hurry to lose money, but do not want to take the time necessary to learn how to make it.

Tradingschool.com uses a combination of biofeedback protocols to accomplish biomechanical training. This training requires complex and precise instrumentation. The equipment is sensitive enough to detect biological electrical activity at minute levels. The detection of various biofeedback information is accomplished by placing sensors or electrodes at specific sites on the human body. These sensors monitor brain waves, muscle tone, blood pressure, and temperature. Not until the mid-1960s did so-called modern medical science realize that a human could control the involuntary or autonomic nervous system. Until that time, scientists did not believe you could control your heartbeat or blood flow. We know now that through training it is possible to accomplish control of an extraordinary kind. Figure 7.2 shows a photograph of sensor placement.

Figure 7.2   Sensor placement

Tradingschool.com uses portable biofeedback equipment instead of a desktop system. The portable notebook computer allows the operator access to various locations and trading environments and has the power to perform all of the tasks necessary in training the biomechanical trader. Two of its features are an active matrix screen and sound. Both visual and auditory information are important in training biomechanical traders. (Figure 7.3 shows the notebook computer and screen.)

The notebook computer is connected to a biofeedback machine. This machine sends the biofeedback information to the computer, where it is processed. It is impossible for someone not trained in biofeedback to operate this equipment. This is why the *contact team* approach is vital to biomechanical training. It is impossible for the student to operate and monitor the equipment. In the first few months of training, the team works closely together. After reprogramming has taken place, the student works independently and meets with the operator once or twice a month. (See photograph of the biofeedback machine in Figure 7.4.)

Figure 7.3 Notebook computer

Figure 7.4   Biofeedback machine

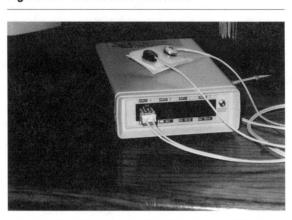

After the student is able to attain the alpha and theta states on his or her own, biofeedback equipment is not necessary. The use of this equipment and other training techniques enable tradingschool .com to achieve in a short period of time what may take years to accomplish without it. Using technology to improve human ability is the ultimate goal. Biomechanical traders know and understand that success lies within them. Once you have mastered the ability to control yourself, you become the ultimate human trading machine.

Deel Mental Conditioning

The use of hypnosis and biofeedback is by no means all there is to the creation of a biomechanical trader. *Deel mental conditioning,* named after the creator of biomechanical training, is to a large extent responsible for traders achieving emotional and physical control so quickly. While the exact process and sequence are proprietary to tradingschool.com, I will explain some of the protocols in the conditioning process.

Flash Recognition
All of us at one time or another have closed our eyes and visualized an image in minute detail. This happens in some cases when we awaken from a dream. We remember the visual image as though we

were looking directly at it with our eyes. Instead, we are seeing with our mind because our eyes are closed. The ability to hold visual information and examine it in detail is of great importance to traders. Trading involves technical analysis and price patterns, all of which are forms of graphic information. If you have the ability to process this information quickly and see what only a trained eye can see, you have an advantage over conventional traders.

The eye views the visual information and sends this information to the brain, where it is then stored. The problem lies in recalling the visual information. What if it were possible to train your eye and brain to act like a digital camera whereby you could view the information at an accelerated rate and be able to recall specific details about the image? This would give you a distinct advantage, because you could gather information faster, process the information, and make an expeditious decision. This ability would enable you to react faster than your competition.

The process begins with the trader sitting in a comfortable chair. A projector flashes a chart pattern that remains on the screen for only four seconds. The trader must identify the pattern and the appropriate course of action a trader should take. To do this, the trader must identify support and resistance, direction of trend, future price direction, volume, and so forth. In the beginning, only one chart is displayed. Information is verbally transmitted by the trader to the operator. After a few sessions, several charts are flashed, one after another. The trader must identify them in order and relay the information to the operator. In a few weeks, distractions are introduced and the recognition time is lowered from four seconds to two seconds. This exercise makes that trader acutely aware of price patterns, momentum, trend, and other trading information. In learning this new skill, the trader is improving recall memory and learning to concentrate intensely without being distracted by outside factors. This enables the trader to make decisions much faster and to trade with confidence.

Visualization

Visualization is a technique to help the trader become synchronized with market momentum and trend. This awareness is on both conscious and subconscious levels. Traders described as super-traders will be overheard to say, "I *feel* the market." Many times they will feel the market going up or down. If you ask them why they feel this way, they will respond, "I don't know, it is just a *feeling* I have." What they are doing without their conscious knowledge is picking up on hidden trends and short-term cycle movements within a market or stock. Visualization is a learned discipline taught at tradingschool.com to merge the trader with market movement.

In visualization training, the trader is shown two curved lines oscillating up and down through each other. After watching the rhythm and momentum for a few minutes, you close your eyes and visualize the pattern in your mind. When you open your eyes the oscillating movements are the same as the picture in your mind. After doing this exercise several times, the speed of the oscillation is changed. You are allowed to view this change for six seconds. After that, you are instructed to close your eyes and push a button when you feel the two lines cross. When you push the button, a white dot appears, marking the spot. In the beginning the dots are well off the mark of the two crossing oscillating lines. In a short time, the dots are on or very close to the mark where the lines cross.

This is only a brief preview of the visualization training process available at tradingschool.com. Visualization leads to another step in the process of Deel Mental Conditioning known as *market awareness and virtual reality.*

Market Awareness

This is a trading simulation based on bar charts and momentum. Traders are asked to observe price momentum for a few minutes. Then they are asked the direction of the next series of bar price movements and express their feeling regarding the direction. This exercise is one of the last steps in the training of a biomechanical trader. The results after completion of months of training is just plain spooky. The biomechanical trader in most cases is able to feel the direction of the movement and, in some cases, how far it will go. There is *nothing* supernatural or psychic about this ability. The biomechanical trader has been trained to observe, remember, focus, and to use his or her mental ability in ways that most people never experience.

A new dimension currently being added to visualization training should be ready to launch by September of the year 2001. The added dimension is *virtual reality*. It will be possible for the trader to step into the market and view the price action as though he or she were part of the market. You will be able to view a price bar forming in three dimensions and walk around it. You will also hear buying and selling and visually see momentum speed up and slow down as you stand on a price bar. You will be able to move from one place on the bar to another or jump to a price bar, moving average, trendline, or volume. This experience will for the first time make you truly *feel* the market. This will enable tradingschool.com to show the biomechanical trader difficult market relationships and concepts. You will see, feel, and hear the market come to life before your very eyes.

The New Biomechanical Trader

Most of this book has been about the new technology of electronic trading. There is no doubt in my mind that for several years electronic traders will have an advantage. The speed and power of trading electronically is far superior to that of online trading. However, success now and in the future does not rest with the latest technology. I think you now understand that success is achieved by the improvement of the trader. The new biomechanical trader is the next step in trading evolution. Few traders will match the success of the biomechanical trader who uses technology as a tool and the enhanced ability described in this chapter. You have a decision to make in this new millennium. It is very simple: Are you going to trade the same way everybody else has for the last 100 years, or are you going to evolve into the new biomechanical trader? What are you going to do? The future awaits your decision.

chapter 8

seize the day

In all probability, the only thing standing in the way of your success is you. Trading and aggressive investing in all their forms are simply roads that lead to an ultimate destination. If you allow yourself to become distracted, you will never complete the journey and never truly reach your goal. On this journey you will encounter many difficulties, but if you keep focused on your goal, success can be yours. Success does, however, have a price. To succeed as a trader or aggressive investor, you are going to have to work very hard. It has been my experience in training thousands of professionals and individuals that the truly successful are willing to work very hard and endure a great deal to reach their goals. Successful people are driven people and do not make excuses. They make it happen. The truth is, most people simply will not put in the necessary time and work or spend the money to educate themselves. Most people want to be successful, but only if it is easy, inexpensive, and convenient. It is no secret that many traders and aggressive investors fail because they are not willing to do what it takes. Success is directly proportional to the amount of *work* you are willing to do that no one else will. Action is what counts. You can talk about trading forever, but success comes only when you stop talking and say to yourself, "I am willing to do whatever it takes, and I accept the hard road I have to walk to reach my destination." In that instant, you gain control of your life, envision your future, and discern what it has to offer you. Reach out your hand, *seize the day*, and never let go.

Not Even on a Silver Platter

What if you were given the opportunity to be personally trained by a leading trading expert? Would you take it? What if that training included an opportunity to be mentored for one year and, if you demonstrated ability and skill, you would be offered capital to trade? Would you do it? In 1998 that is exactly what I offered. I called it my "trading scholarship program." I was looking for talented traders. I had been hearing for years that all they needed was a break. There were only three requirements:

1. They had to be over 18 years of age.
2. They had to successfully complete four specific trading-school.com courses.
3. They had to demonstrate skill and ability in trading.

If any individual met these three requirements, I would arrange for them to have capital to trade. How much? If they showed the ability to trade and followed the trading plan, over $1 million. Oh, I forgot to mention, they would keep 90 percent of the profits. I estimate that well over 200,000 people in the Los Angeles area heard me make this offer, and I repeated it over a period of five months. How many people do you think enrolled in the trading scholarship program? Read the offer again and guess how many applied. I was personally shocked by the number of people who applied. For some people, this offer was literally the chance of a lifetime. Opportunity knocks only once or twice in life, and if you do not open the door it goes away. How many took the opportunity? Would you have been one of them? How many do you think took advantage of this once-in-a-lifetime opportunity? The answer is *one*. No, this is not a misprint. One person followed through. I could not believe it.

You see, even when an opportunity is offered on a silver platter, the majority of people will not take the time or do the work necessary to be successful, not even for $1 million.

Your Trading Room

One of the keys to being a successful trader is a well-organized trading room. This room is the most important room in your house or office. You will need to take time to design the most efficient trading area possible. In Chapter 7 you learned about the need for natural light and properly controlled room temperature. You also learned about the distractions of repetitious noise. Your trading room needs to have a lot of thought put into it before you start buying computers and bringing in phone lines. Let's start from the beginning.

Power Outlets

Are there enough power outlets in the room, and are they positioned appropriately? If you move into a new home or office, before you connect any electrical devices, check the electrical outlets. It is very simple to do this with a three-pronged circuit analyzer. You simply plug it in and it tells you whether you will fry your computer system or other electrical devices. This little $5 device saved me from destroying my computer system. If you are going to install any kind of electrical equipment, first check the power outlets with a circuit analyzer.

Shape of the Room

If possible, measure the room you intend to use for trading. After completing the measurements, think about the position of your desks, computers, printers, phone, filing cabinets, and so forth. The shape of the room is important because in all probability you will be using a multimonitor configuration of at least two, possibly four monitors. Placing them in the right area, away from glare, and in a visually efficient configuration is critical. All of this will depend on the size and shape of your room. I know a trader who went out and bought a beautiful $1,500 oak computer desk combination. The only problem was that the shape of his room required a triangular corner unit, which would not fit through a normal-size door. If you can measure and map out your trading room before you buy furniture or computers, you will be ahead of the game. If the room is empty, place tape on the floor to outline the desk and other office equipment. This will allow you to scope out possible problems before they arise. You might also use graph paper to draw the room and furniture to scale. Try to find the largest, best-lighted room you can for your trading room.

Lighting

If possible, your trading room should have a window. You want natural light. If this is not possible, arrange for overhead light with natural light panels. Avoid desk lamps if at all possible. They tend to create glare and extra heat in the room. If you have to have a desk light, make sure it lights your desk area without creating eyestrain or causing reflections off of the monitor screens.

Work Area

You need as much work area on your desk as possible for charts, books, and written materials. First measure from the front of your monitors to the wall. Once you have positioned the monitors in the configuration you desire, you will need an additional 15 inches (minimum) of desk space in front of them. The more work area the better. Every aspect of your trading room must be carefully designed.

Wall space can be used effectively for storage shelves and corkboards for displaying information. One whole wall in my office is dedicated as a bookshelf and storage area. Make sure you have a paper shredder in your office so your desk is not covered with an endless blizzard of white paper.

Desk and Trading Array

Figure 8.1 shows a photograph of my trading room, which has plenty of light and work space. The printer and other equipment are well positioned to be easily accessible from the center of the trading desk. You will also notice that I have three 19-inch monitors. Your trading room can greatly contribute to how efficiently you process informa-

Figure 8.1   Desk and trading array

tion. Trading is all about seeing as much information as you can at a glance and acting upon it. If your room is not set up efficiently, you could actually lose money because of poor design. Figure 8.1 will give you an idea of one type of trading room configuration.

The Trading Array   There are three popular trading array configurations. Two-, three-, and four-monitor arrays are the most common. Let us take a look at these three setups.

1. *Two-monitor array*

In the two-monitor array setup, the monitors are set at an angle to each other. Make sure that you can see everything on both screens and that no glare reflects off the monitors. After half an hour of exposure, glare can cause your eyes to burn and may initiate a blinking reflex. If the monitors physically touch, it is possible that electromagnetic flux lines will form near where they meet. The lines are visible as black circular patterns near the edge of the screen. In some cases, you can avoid this by keeping them 1½ inches apart.

2. *Three-monitor array*

◯←You

The three-monitor array is, in my opinion, the ideal configuration. You have enough visual real estate to place your various trading software in windows that are easy to see. The scale of your visual information is important and usually overlooked. Larger charts are better. A typical bar chart with intraday data should be at least 4 inches long and 3¼ inches high. Your physical distance from the trading array is also important. In a three-monitor configuration, while sitting in the middle of the array, you should be able to extend your left arm to the far right and move it in an arc in front of you without touching the screens. The screens should be 3 inches from your finger tips. This distance will enable you to see all three screens with very little movement your head. (If you are constantly moving your head from side to side, in less than an hour you will develop a neckache and possibly a headache.) The three screens should be visible and well within your peripheral vision. A simple yet effective way of correctly placing the array is to sit at the desk where you are going to set up the three screens and extend your arms to form a V shape. Looking straight ahead, you should be able to see both of your hands.

3. *Four-monitor array*

— — — —

()←You

Most likely, you will never need four monitors. It does, however, give you a feeling of power and invincibility. Just remember, you can lose money whether you trade with four monitors or one. If you are going to use four monitors, do not stack them one on top of another and do not arrange an array that forces you to tilt your head upward. Place the monitors so that they are on eye level. Quite often, new traders will buy a large conference table and place all four monitors in a line with themselves in the middle. This is fine; however, most traders sit too close to the monitors. To see all four monitors, they have to swing their heads from right to left all through the trading day. If you use the four-monitor setup, sit back far enough to enable you to see all of the monitors with very little movement of your head.

Is Bigger Better? There is very little reason to purchase a 21-inch monitor. The pure size and weight of the monitor makes it very cumbersome. If you ever have to have it repaired, moving it could break your back, and if that does not do it the repair bill will. It takes up so much desk space that you have almost no work area. You may have to move out so your 21-inch monitor will have a place to live. There are cost-effective monitors on the market that give you a large visual area and do not hog the work space on your desk. I suggest you look at the ViewSonic PS 790 monitor. It is a 19-inch monitor, but takes up only the space of a 15-inch monitor. Always try to buy as much visual real estate as you can without having it take over your desk.

As of yet, the flat-panel screens do not have the resolution or dot pitch necessary to justify the cost. In at least one instance, the repair costs on one flat-panel monitor were more than the price of a 17-inch monitor. In the future, the flat-panel or wall-mounted super-screens will be the answer, but that is still a few years away. Now let us consider other factors.

Other Factors When you are looking for monitors for your trading array, you will want them to have the capability to achieve very high resolutions. I suggest they have the ability to reach a screen resolution of 1280×1024 or 1600×1200. Another factor is the dot pitch. Dot pitch is responsible for the clear images. A dot pitch of 0.25 to 0.26 will give you superclear images. Your monitors should also have the ability to reset to different refresh rates. Higher refresh rates are better for your eyes. If, after the trading day, your eyes itch and burn, more than likely it is because of your monitor's dot pitch and low refresh rate. When it comes to your trading array, spend the money necessary get the best monitors you can. You will probably spend from $350 to $550 for each monitor. Believe me, it is worth it just to avoid itchy, burning eyes at the end of the trading day. As with all trading equipment, remember to spend your money on tools, not toys. Toys will cost a lot more in the long run. Figure 8.2 shows a photo of a three-monitor configuration.

Graphics Cards

You are better off buying one graphics card that will run four monitors at one time. While Windows 98 will run multiple monitors, most traders who use it seem to have problems with it crashing. I suggest you consider Colorgraphic. This company manufactures professional graphics cards, and it has a fine reputation and offers multiple products. Before you buy a computer, find out about its ability to drive multiple monitors. Call Colorgraphic's toll-free number (1-887-WIDE VIEW), or visit its Web site at www.colorgraphic.net.

Modems and High-Speed Connections

Depending on where you live, you will have various options. I use a cable modem and an ISDN line as a backup. Speed is everything, so you will want to test the speed of your connection. It does not make any sense at all to do all the analysis only to hit the buy or sell button and have the order take an eternity. Whichever technology you use, make sure you thoroughly investigate your options, especially

Figure 8.2 Three-monitor configuration

with DSL and ADSL. Where you live will determine the type and availability of the high-speed access you have.

Computer Requirements

At www.tradingschool.com, we build *custom computers* for our student traders. We offer these systems at just over cost as a service to our students. Here is a list of the *minimum* requirements:

The fastest processor currently available

128MB of RAM

10- to 14-Gig hard drive

40× CD-ROM or DVD

1.44 floppy drive

Backup at your discretion

Colorgraphic card

512K cache

Sound card

Speakers

56K modem

Microsoft or Logitech mouse, no trackball

Backup power supply

The Chair

When you trade you need a comfortable chair with lots of back support. Whatever you do, buy the best chair that fits your needs. Do not try to save money by buying a cheap pincushion chair. You are going to be spending not just hours but literally days in that chair. Buy the best chair you can. If your back hurts after long hours of trading, you might want to think about buying a new chair with better support.

tradingschool.com

To be a successful trader, you are going to need educational support. You will never learn how to successfully trade from reading a book. This book and others offer ideas and information, but you also need hands-on education from professionals who train other professionals. Tradingschool.com is a true trading school that teaches the art and science of trading and aggressive investing. Realizing that you need professional guidance from an *independent educational company* that has no vested interest in the number of times you trade is the first step toward success.

Tradingschool.com trains day traders, short-term momentum traders, and aggressive investors. Students come to trading-school.com from all over the United States and around the world to improve their trading skills. Regardless of whether you are a beginner or an experienced trader, tradingschool.com's hands-on work-shops, online courses, and educational materials can assist you in your quest for knowledge and experience.

Tradingschool.com will train you to become a high-probability, profitability trader. It is quite likely that you will learn trading strate-gies and methodologies that you will not learn elsewhere because of the company's independence and allegiance to the students.

At tradingschool.com you will learn state-of-the-art technology, strategy, and techniques used by professional traders. Trading-school.com has the distinction of offering biomechanical training and conditioning. Tradingschool.com "trains the minds that trade the markets." You may contact tradingschool.com at

tradingschool.com
P.O. Box 1831
Duarte, CA 91010
Phone 626-963-2057
www.tradingschool.com

In the final analysis, *you* are responsible for your success or fail-ure. You and only you can decide to walk the road seldom traveled. Once you reach the final destination, you will have the satisfaction of knowing that you are living the dream instead of dreaming it.

index